Why Julian Now?

A Voyage of Discovery

SHEILA UPJOHN

DARTON·LONGMAN + TODD

First published 1997 by
Darton, Longman and Todd Ltd
1 Spencer Court
140–142 Wandsworth High Street
London SW18 4JJ

ISBN 0–232–52217–0

A catalogue record for this book is available
from the British Library.

Designed by Sandie Boccacci
Phototypeset in 9^1/$_4$/13 pt Palatino by Intype London Ltd
Printed and bound in Great Britain by Page Bros, Norwich

This book is for the
Community of All Hallows
Ditchingham
in whose Gate House
much of it was written

I am most grateful to Alan Oldfield, the Australian artist who has shown me so much about Julian, for once again allowing me to use one of his paintings in the series *Revelations of Divine Love of Julian of Norwich* for the cover illustration.

CONTENTS

INTRODUCTION

A Voyage of Discovery

THIS BOOK WAS begun because I was always being asked a question I could not answer. Time and again, when I went to speak on Julian, someone would ask, 'Could you tell me why it is that suddenly so many people are reading Julian of Norwich?'

I would always give some sort of answer, but the more I was asked, the less satisfactory my answer appeared. In the end I realised that there must be, not one answer to the question, but very many – and that, unless I set out to try to discover what they were, I should, as Julian says, 'be always wanting'.

So, seven years after I had first set off *In Search of Julian of Norwich*, I found myself embarking once more on a voyage of discovery. This time the object of my search was to try to discover where it was that some of the answers to that question *Why Julian Now?* were to be found.

It is a journey on which I have abandoned maps and tried to be guided by Julian's own lantern, shining ahead of me. It has taken me to many strange places, some of which – given the choice – I should not have chosen to visit. In all of them I found buried treasure. This book is a collection of the traveller's tales I wrote on that journey.

CHAPTER ONE

The Start of the Journey

ONCE UPON a time, which is the start of all good stories, I used to reply to the question 'Why Julian now?' by saying that it was, perhaps, because her age and ours are similar. We have wars, plagues, violence and uncertainty in our century, just as she did in the turbulent fourteenth century. And so this might be why we respond so eagerly today to what she has to say.

It always seemed to me a very plausible answer – and I found it was quite labour-saving, too – because if you assume that it is because things are the same, there's no need to spend time finding out what is different. It was only by chance (though Julian says nothing happens by chance) that something happened to make me realise that it probably was not true.

It was a dark wet night in February. The entry in my diary – 'Lecture on roof bosses of Norwich Cathedral 7.30' – looked unappealing. I decided to put another log on the fire and finish the whisky instead. Then a little voice in my head reminded me: 'You finished the whisky *last* night.' So I got out the car and went. Little did I think it was to be the start of a much longer journey.

The lecture, by Martial Rose, was an eye-opener. As a result, we later worked together to make a video of the roof bosses in the cloisters. And it was while we were filming it that I realised that, when the first bosses were being carved, Julian was writing her book less than a mile away in King Street.

These first bosses mark an artistic breakthrough. They begin, in the east walk, with conventional foliage. Then green men and dragons begin to peep out of the leaves. Suddenly the leaves are curled back to reveal a series of sculptures that tell the story of Christ's Passion. They tell it in sequence – a kind of strip cartoon in stone. It is an astonishing development, an entirely new art form, and there is nothing like it anywhere in the world.

It was then that I first began to question that plausible and labour-saving answer. 'Perhaps we have the wars and violence,' I thought, 'but nothing remotely like *this* is happening in our century.' So, instead of letting dates just swim before my eyes, as they generally do, I took the date of Julian's birth – 1342 – and the date of her death – say, 1420 – and used them as a window through which to view the creative activity in Norwich during those years. I found that those astounding cloister bosses were a drop in the ocean. In Julian's day, the square mile of the walled city of Norwich held another twenty-one religious houses, as well as the cathedral, together with no less than sixty-three parish churches. During her lifetime nearly all of them were being enlarged and refurbished. Norwich people were at work painting frescoes, and rood screens, and altar pieces. They were carving in wood and in stone – bosses and tracery and saints and fonts and angel-roofs and misericords. They were embroidering sumptuous vestments and altar frontals. They were designing and making stained glass: the Norwich workshops were famous. Norwich goldsmiths and silversmiths were making chalices and pattens. Scribes were illuminating manuscripts. They were building churches in daring and original styles. The place was alive with people making beautiful things.

I realised that it is only because of the orgy of destruction ordered first by Henry VIII and then by Oliver Cromwell that we no longer appreciate how much of it there was, as well as how beautiful it is. And as I looked, with new eyes, at the few glorious fragments that are left, it seemed to me that, though the exterior world of the people who created it might have been as violent and unsettled as our own, they must have had a quite different interior world that helped them make sense of it.

For I had to recognise the fact that these beautiful things were made by a handful of illiterate craftsmen who were poorly fed, badly housed, and who had a life expectancy of no more fifty; that they were created in spite of the fact that the young men were being shipped off to die in the futile war in France; that ruinous taxes were being imposed to pay for it; that outbreaks of cattle disease meant hunger, and disastrous harvests meant starvation – so that desperate peasants stormed Norwich, looting and killing – and were themselves brutally put to death. And I also had to accept the fact that, three times in Julian's lifetime, so many people died in outbreaks of the Black Death that work sometimes had to be abandoned altogether.

How should we react today, I wondered, if a third of the population died within the space of months, so that we ran out of space to bury the dead and of priests to conduct the funerals? Should we find ourselves serenely carving roof bosses and painting frescoes? It seemed to me more likely that a second epidemic would follow on the heels of the first – an epidemic of panic and terror and despair.

Yet – apart from a few macabre Dance of Deaths – I could find no evidence of terror and despair in the art. I could not believe that all this beauty was the work of people who felt that life was spinning out of control. To me it looked like the work of secure and mature people who have a grasp of their true nature, and whose world picture enabled them to make sense of the horrors surrounding them.

For art does, I believe, reflect both our age and the way we see ourselves. I thought of the way Greek art and architecture reflects the maturity of their philosophy, and of the way that Roman art and architecture – where gladiatorial contests, not high drama, took place in the amphitheatres – is subtly coarser. I thought of the monstrous buildings and statues that sprang out of Communism, and of the monolithic buildings of Nazi Germany and Fascist Italy. And so I thought, if I was going to compare Julian's century with our own, I should start by looking at our late-twentieth-century art and see what I could discover from it.

As I passed the wilder shores of modern art I saw dismembered cows and piles of bricks. There seemed no common ground between them and the art of Julian's day and I decided to sail on. But I decided I must make landfall on the rocky promontory that is Francis Bacon, for he has been hailed by many critics as the most important and original artist of the twentieth century. So I read what the art critic Richard Dorment, who admires Bacon's work, said when he wrote Bacon's obituary (*Daily Telegraph*, 29th April 1992):

> What made Bacon's work so chilling was that there was no softening of the despair, no diminution of the ferocious loathing for the human condition . . . There was a grandeur in Bacon's art because his theme was a terrible one: a revulsion against his own humanity. He turned self-hatred into high art.

I was interested when I read this because, not long before, the annual Julian lecture in Norwich had been given by Brian Thorne, a practising psychotherapist. In it, he had suggested that self-hatred and a revulsion against our own humanity was fast becoming the typical response to life in our day. If he was right, it seemed to me that Francis Bacon's claim to greatness might well rest on the fact that, as great artists do, he faithfully reflected the spirit of the age we live in.

For I was beginning to have a suspicion that the reason why Julian's book is so important today is that her century was – not similar – but completely different from our own. So I thought I had better start by looking, not at the events of her time, but at her interior world picture. How did Julian see our place in the world, and where did she think we came from? And, with sinking heart, I realised that I was heading straight for the Garden of Eden.

CHAPTER TWO

Voyage towards That Other Eden

THE GARDEN of Eden was the last place I had imagined I should visit on my voyage to discover why Julian's book seems to speak so clearly to us today. Yet, for Julian, the creation story in Genesis was the start of history. She believed that God made Adam and Eve in his own image, and that he looked on his work and saw that it was good; that there was a garden called Eden with a tree whose fruit Adam and Eve were forbidden to eat; that the serpent persuaded Eve to eat the fruit, that Eve then persuaded Adam, and as a result they were both turned out of Paradise.

This didn't somehow seem to me to be a very compelling reason for her book being relevant today. The story had, after all, been comprehensively discredited in 1859 when *The Origin of Species* was published. At that date our great-grandfathers had been mortified to discover that there was no Garden of Eden, no forbidden fruit, no serpent – and that, far from our first parents being Adam and Eve, we were all descended from monkeys. They lost even more face when it transpired that – whoever made the world – it took an awful lot longer than six days to do it. And they were so humiliated at being caught out taking a myth for a fact that they had reacted by covering their shame – not with fig leaves – but by turning their backs on the whole story.

However, once Julian had led me back to Eden, I began to realise

8

that one of the great losses of our age has been the way we subject everything to the limitations of scientific thinking, so that we no longer seem to have any idea of the difference between truth and fact.

One of the many things I believe, for instance, is that when Eurydice was killed by a serpent's sting, her grieving husband Orpheus went down to Hades – across the Styx and past the damned in their torments – into the depths of hell. His music was so beautiful that the dark god of Hades relented. He allowed Eurydice to follow Orpheus out of hell on one condition – that he did not look back. And that at the very mouth of hell Orpheus's faith failed. He looked back – and saw Eurydice being snatched away from him back into the darkness. The story laid hold on my imagination when I first read it, as a child of perhaps eight, and I knew then – and know now – that somehow it is my job to make the same journey, and to reach the end of that tunnel without turning back. Perhaps the story is an allegory of faith. I don't know. But I do know that it is true, and I shall continue to believe it – no matter how many well-intentioned scientists tap me kindly on the shoulder and tell me it never happened.

It was also becoming clear to me that, although we do not openly acknowledge it, we have recently developed a strange double standard about myths. It seems to be becoming received opinion that nineteenth-century Christian missionaries were interfering busybodies who did more harm than good because they destroyed belief in the life-enhancing myths of the people they sought to convert. But no one, as far as I could see, has anything but admiration for those ardent nineteenth-century rationalists whose literal-minded bigotry did so much to destroy belief in the life-sustaining truths of Christianity. For it is because those eminent Victorians were so mightily embarrassed that we have lost our grasp of the enormous truths of the Eden story.

But no people can exist without a myth about their first begin-

9

nings. And so, if our century has abandoned Julian's belief in the story of Adam and Eve, I reasoned that it must have been necessary for us to construct another, an alternative, creation story and another Eden. And so I set out to see if I could discover it.

It's not an easy place to find. There are no charts. For whereas the fourteenth-century Paradise could be reached through reliable directions set out in a Book and a Creed, the course to the Paradise of the secular society has to be sought through a fog of cloudy ideals and the shoals of unwritten assumptions. To make matters worse, I could only test the validity of these assumptions against fourteenth-century data.

And here I had to acknowledge that, as far as their physical world picture was concerned, the fourteenth-century had been guilty, let's face it, of what one might call some major geographical inexactitudes. They believed the earth was flat and the sun revolved round it. If they were wrong about that, why should their ethical directions be any more trustworthy? Surely Julian's instructions on how to find the way to Paradise had long passed their 'believe-by' date and must be dumped?

It was while I was struggling with these discouraging thoughts that I was greatly cheered to read what C. S. Lewis says about what he calls 'chronological snobbery' in *Surprised by Joy.*

> Chronological snobbery is the uncritical acceptance of the intellectual climate common to our own age and the assumption that whatever has gone out of date is on that account discredited. You must find out *why* it went out of date. Was it ever refuted (and if so by whom; where and how conclusively?) or did it merely die away as fashions do? If this latter, this tells us nothing about its truth or falsehood. From seeing this, one passes to the realisation that our own age is also 'a period', and certainly has, like all periods, its characteristic illusions. They are likeliest to lurk in those wide-spread

10

assumptions which are so ingrained in the age that no one dares either to attack them or feels it necessary to defend them.[1]

It seemed to me that these assumptions might well point the way to the new Garden of Eden, and so, if I could identify them and follow where they led, I should eventually arrive. And I kept finding that, like Alice in *Through The Looking Glass*, I was always walking in at the same door. That door is the late-eighteenth-century document 'The American Declaration of Independence' – part of which reads:

> *We hold these truths to be self-evident, that all men are created equal, that they are endowed by their Creator with certain unalienable rights, that among these are life, liberty and the pursuit of happiness. – That to secure these rights, Governments are instituted among Men, deriving their just powers from the consent of the governed.*

The more I considered it, the more I was surprised to find that what was intended simply as a political document, in fact proposes nothing less than an alternative view of creation ' . . . *created equal . . . endowed by their Creator with certain unalienable rights*'. It is a view that is completely at variance with Julian's and, before I set it alongside hers, I thought it might be a good idea to see when and why it was written.

The Declaration was drawn up a year after the American colonies had risen in revolt, and the war was going against them. The day the Declaration was signed, 4th July 1776, the British Fleet had sailed into New York Harbour and was at that very moment setting up camp on Staten Island ready to attack – and later take – New York. It is a backs-to-the-wall statement to justify a political rebellion.

---

1. Fontana, 1959, Ch. 13, p. 196

For although the new ideas of the Enlightenment were sweeping the intellectual world, Thomas Paine's *Rights of Man* was not to be published for another fourteen years, and the storming of the Bastille lay – almost to the day – thirteen years in the future. The assertions so confidently put forward are not the proven pronouncements of a new school of philosophy, but primarily a defence against a capital charge of treason. First and foremost the Declaration is a political document.

But political documents – however well-intentioned – are not holy writ, and it is very dangerous to confuse the two. And I was beginning to have an uneasy feeling that we subsequently had been behaving as if the Declaration of Independence version of the creation story was written on tablets of stone.

I also realised that, for all its assertion that all men are created equal, some were manifestly treated more equally than others in the land of the free. It was to take another 100 years before negroes could no longer legally be bought and sold as slaves in America – and their emancipation was so fiercely opposed that it took a bloody Civil War to achieve it. So the Declaration is not a factual account of the way things are, but a manifesto of aspirations and ideals. What's more, I realised that this alternative view of creation hangs, not on any new scientific proof, but on the concept of 'a self-evident truth', which means 'because I say so'. And, in turn, all this meant that the new story of creation, while it might or might not be true, had no more basis in fact than Julian's.

So then I had to ask myself which view of creation fitted the facts of life as I saw them. Were we 'created equal' and endowed with 'certain unalienable rights' – or were we created in God's image, the heirs of Adam and Eve, and inheritors of a fallen world? And I had to admit that, of the two myths, Julian's seemed to me by far the more convincing.

At this point, when I realised I had reached the high ground from which I was going to have to declare that I believe in the Garden of Eden and do not believe in human rights, I became a little worried. People reading this, it seemed to me, would decide that my journey had taken me to that island where people lose their wits, and it would not be long before they sent the kind men in white coats to take me away in a plain van. So I looked round, desperately hoping there might be someone else in this neck of the woods. And there was. Thomas Merton. I felt like running into the streets in a bath towel shouting '*Eureka!*' when I found these words staring up at me from the pages of his *Conjectures of a Guilty Bystander*.

> The discovery of America – this belief in the obvious possibilities of an immense new continent, a place fabulously endowed and blessed, had fantastic potency. It galvanised and inebriated the Western world. It did more than anything else – even Copernicus and Galileo – to overturn the world view of the Middle Ages [Julian's world view, that is]. It revolutionised the thought of Western man. He was now convinced that human society was getting off *to an entirely new start* . . .
>
> The New-Found-Land was a world *without history,* therefore without sin, therefore a paradise. To this world came the victims of a Europe grown old in wickedness, with a history of arbitrary authority. To escape from history – that is to say from Europe, to escape from the burden of the past, to return to the source, to begin again a new history, starting off from scratch, *without original sin.* This is what America offered to the oppressed, the persecuted, the unsuccessful – or the merely discontented . . .
>
> The Indian could somehow seem to be the serpent in Paradise, because he was outside the myth, for he is older, he was there before, he had roots in the ground when we arrived.

Whereas we arrived suddenly, we stepped off the Mayflower in perfect innocence, for we had left all our sins in the ocean.[2]

This new story of 'Paradise Never Lost' was, it seemed to me, written between the lines of the Declaration of Independence. It read something like this: 'Forget the Fall – it never happened. Man is in his rightful place in the earthly Paradise and, this time round, he is endowed by his Creator not with an opportunity to stand or fall – but with "certain rights" which the government he chooses has a duty to secure for him. Everything in the garden is lovely.'

I had arrived at that other Eden, demi-Paradise – and now I had to go back to Julian's Eden so I could compare the two of them and see if I could discover which of these Paradises stood on the good earth, and which was an unreal island of cloud-capped fantasy.

2. Burns & Oates, 1995, pp. 34–9

CHAPTER THREE

Black Holes and Double Vision

WHEN I GOT back to Eden, nothing had changed. In Julian's world God still made Adam and Eve in his own image, and he looked on his work and saw that it was good. There was a garden and a tree of forbidden fruit. The serpent persuaded Eve to eat the fruit and Eve then persuaded Adam. As a result they were turned out of Paradise.

Could *this* be why we read Julian, I asked myself? For these antiquated and exploded myths? Could it be *this* that made her century able to withstand the disasters and misery that beset them? Surely the notion that man is created with a right to life, liberty and the pursuit of happiness is so very much more cheerful and attractive a view of life that it has got to be true. Then I remembered something I had read in Dorothy L. Sayers' *The Mind of the Maker*:

> The proper question to be asked about any creed, is not 'Is it pleasant?' but, 'Is it true?' . . . The necessary condition for assessing the value of creeds is that we should fully understand that they claim to be, not idealistic fancies, not arbitrary codes, not abstractions irrelevant to human life and thought, but statements of fact about the universe as we know it.[1]

So the question I now had to ask myself was whether the notion

---

1. Harper & Row, 1979, Ch. 1, p. 16

that we are created equal and with a right to happiness is a statement of fact, or if it is an idealistic fantasy. For, if it were to turn out to be nothing but an idealistic fantasy, then it was not surprising that, if we based our expectations on it, it would make us a prey to self-hatred and despair.

The reason it should do so, it seemed to me, was something like this: if we have a right to pursue happiness, we (presumably) also have a right to capture it – otherwise what's the point of pursuing it? This means that anything that makes us *unhappy* is seen, not as something to be made the best of, but as a frustration of our proper expectations and our rights. So unhappiness is no longer something to be endured by the fallen children of Eve in a fallen world, but something that should not have been allowed to occur – and that means *somebody's fault*.

Then I considered the accusatory style of journalism that seems to have become our commonplace way of reacting to disasters, and thought it showed that I was in the right place. For nowadays, let a train be derailed, an earthquake occur, an epidemic strike or an aeroplane crash, and the newspapers are full of guilt-ascribing articles. On television, politicians and officials are hauled before the cameras to give an account of their stewardship and confess their failures. Culprits are identified and enormous sums of money are then claimed in compensation from those held to be responsible.

So I began to suspect that, strange as it might seem, substituting the Rights of Man for the Fall of Man multiplies guilt, rather than abolishes it. For this world is manifestly not an earthly Paradise – and now we no longer have an explanation of why it's not. We look uneasily round for a culprit, and, if we cannot identify one, we may begin to feel in some obscure way 'we are all guilty'.

Pondering on this, I came across what Brian Thorne wrote in his introduction to John Michael Mountney's *Sin Shall Be A Glory*:[2] 'I have come to believe that most of us, most of the time, are increasingly caught up in a fearsome web of guilt and, like Kafka's K, we have no clear grasp either of our crimes or of the court in which we stand convicted.' And since Brian Thorne is Director of Student Counselling at the University of East Anglia, as well as being a psychotherapist in general practice, I thought he was well placed to know the besetting anxieties of our time.

And it seemed to me the reason for this shadowy and pervasive *angst* might be that, whereas once we were sinners who could be forgiven, now we are culprits who fail to solve problems. Unfortunately there is no formula for forgiving those who fail to solve problems in the earthly Paradise. The only possible course is to exact retribution.

It was when I was wondering when it was that we started seeing unhappiness as a problem that should have been solved – not as part of the way life is – that I came across this in *The Mind of The Maker*.

It has become abundantly clear of late years that something has gone seriously wrong with our conception of humanity and of humanity's proper attitude to the universe. . . . To the average man, life presents itself, not as material to his hand, but as a series of *problems* of extreme difficulty, which he has to *solve* with the means at his disposal. . . . [Many people now have] a firmly implanted notion that all human situations are 'problems' like detective story problems, capable of a single, necessary and categorical solution, which must be wholly right, while all others are wholly wrong. But this they cannot be, since human situations are subject to the law of human

2. Darton, Longman & Todd, 1992

nature, whose evil is at all times rooted in its good, and whose good can only redeem, but not abolish, its evil.[3]

'Whose evil is at all times rooted in its good, and whose good can only redeem, but not abolish, its evil.' This brought me straight back to Julian. She writes:

> Our blessed Lord answered very gently, with a most kind look, and showed that Adam's sin was the worst harm that was done and ever shall be until the world's end. He also showed this is clearly known by all Holy Church on earth. More than this, he taught me I should look upon the glorious Atonement. For this making amends is more helpful to the salvation of many, without compare, than ever the sin of Adam was harmful.
>
> What our Lord means by this teaching is that we should remember this: 'Since I have brought good out of the worst evil, I want you to know, by this, that I shall bring good out of all lesser evils, too'. (Ch. 29)

As I read Julian's words about the Garden of Eden, I recognised their riches. For built into the myth of the Fall of Man is the concept of good coming out of evil. And it was then that I realised that in the myth of the Rights of Man – which sees evil as something that can, and should, be abolished – the concept has disappeared entirely. For much of the time no one seems to notice it is missing. It is only when we come across a 'problem' that we cannot 'solve' that we fall into the black hole its absence leaves.

Once more I turned to *The Mind of the Maker*:

> There is no solution to death. There is no means by which you or I, by taking thought, can solve this difficulty in such a manner that it no longer exists ... Of late we have noticed

---

3. Ch. 11, p. 179

a growing resentment and exasperation in the face of death. We do not so much fear the pains of dying, as feel affronted by the notion that anything in this world should be inevitable. Our efforts are not directed, like those of the saint or the poet, to make something creative out of the idea of death, but rather to seeing whether we cannot somehow evade, abolish, in fact 'solve the problem' of death.[4]

'A growing resentment and exasperation in the face of death.' This, surely, is what our age demonstrates. I remembered the many times I had seen on television the baffled, angry resentment of parents demanding an operation of horrendous hazards and huge expense for their dying child. I thought of the headline 'Baby Jason Loses Fight for Life' – and realised that nowadays, increasingly, this is the way death is spoken of. And I reflected that all this was designed to conceal the fact that the fight with death – on this level – is one that only one man, anywhere, ever had a chance of winning.

It surprised me to find that Sayers wrote this as long ago as 1940, since it was not until 1967 that Dr Christiaan Barnard carried out the first heart transplant and opened up even more ways to try to cheat the inevitability of death. At the time, it reminded me of Sir Philip Sydney's delightful sonnet 'My true-love has my heart and I have his' and I wrote a companion piece on our despairing efforts to prolong life in the twentieth century.

c.1582

My true-love has my heart and I have his
By just exchange, one for the other given;
I hold his dear and mine he cannot miss,
There never was a better bargain driven.

---

4. p. 195.

His heart in me keeps me and him in one,
My heart in him his thought and senses guides;
He loves my heart, for once it was his own,
I cherish it because in me it bides.
His heart his wound received from my sight,
My heart was wounded with his wounded heart;
For as from me, on him, his hurt did light,
So still, methought, in me his hurt did smart.
Both equal hurt, by this change sought our bliss:
My true-love has my heart, and I have his.

1967

My true-love has my heart. I have not his
For I was dead the day my heart was given.
We made a bargain my heart should be his,
Then, by rash chance, I to my death was driven.
His heart was cut out on the day I died,
My heart, which beat for him, stitched in his breast;
My heart in him his thought and senses guides,
His heart and my poor body are at rest.
So what is life to him, was death to me,
Yet what he takes is what I gladly give.
I should have died hereafter, so will he.
What has he gained by a few years to live?
Bodies are born to die, true loves to part.
Death still waits for him, though he has my heart.

'Bodies are born to die, true loves to part. . . .' They knew that
was true in the centuries before our own, and yet, underpinned
by the teaching of the Church, they could recognise that death can
be swallowed up in victory. Today in the secular society we rage
against the dying of the light. We do not go gentle into that good

night – we fight fill we drop. I began to wonder whether one of
the reasons we read Julian today is simply because she restates the
teaching of the Church clearly and effectively.

Having got this far, I had to admit that there were many things
in her book that would have been completely at variance with the
Church's teaching in her day. But I also had to acknowledge that
Julian says, over and over again, that she was not led away from
the teaching of the Church by the Showings. Some people have
said she protests too much – but I cannot believe, as they do, that
she was making a parade of her loyalty to divert suspicion. I
believe she said it, as she said everything else, because she meant it.

She writes:

> Now during all this time, from beginning to end, I had two
> different kinds of understanding. One was the endless, con-
> tinuing love, with its assurance of safekeeping and joyful
> salvation – for this is the message of all the Showings.
>
> The other was the day-to-day teaching of Holy Church, in
> which I had been taught and grounded, and which I under-
> stood and practised with all my heart. And this was not taken
> away from me, for I was not turned or led away from it at
> any point of the Showings. But I was taught, by this, to love
> it and rejoice in it so that, by the help of our Lord and his
> grace, I might grow and rise through it to more heavenly
> knowledge and higher loving. (Ch. 46)

Before I went any further I had to understand, as Julian did, that
the Church's teaching was being extended, not abolished, and
that she was not a rebel, she was a mystic. And as I struggled to
put into words what a mystic is, I was delighted to find this
definition in G.K. Chesterton's *Orthodoxy*:[5]

The ordinary man has always been sane because the ordinary

---

5. Bodley Head, 1908, Ch. 2, p. 46

man has always been a mystic. He has permitted the twilight . . . He has always cared more for truth than for consistency. If he saw two truths that seemed to contradict each other, he would take the two truths and the contradiction along with them. His spiritual sight is stereoscopic, like his physical sight; he sees two different pictures at once and yet sees all the better for that.

I believe this puts Julian's experience with complete accuracy. Her spiritual sight *is* stereoscopic. She does see 'two different pictures at once and yet sees all the better for that'. And I was beginning to believe it is her refusal to jettison what she can't fit into a neat picture that is one of the many things that commends her to us today. For our view of mankind seems to me to be becoming more and more like the terrible bed of Procrustes that fitted everybody. The giant made it fit by the simple expedient of chopping off the feet of those who were too tall – and stretching on a rack those who were too short.

But for Julian there were no easy answers. Throughout her book she was forced to grapple with two truths that seemed to contradict each other and which she had to reconcile:

'Good Lord, I see that you are truth itself, and I know truly that we sin grievously all the day long and are much to blame. And I can neither forsake knowing this truth, nor do I see you put any blame upon us. How can this be?' For I knew by the teaching of holy church, and by my own feelings, that the blame for our sin lies heavy upon us, from the first man until the time we come up to heaven. This, then, was my wonder – that I saw our Lord putting no more blame upon us than if we were as clean and holy as the angels in heaven.

And my mind was greatly troubled in its blindness by these two contradictions. And I knew no rest, for fear that his blessed presence should pass from my sight and I should be left not knowing how I should look on sin and the nature of our blame. I cried inwardly with all my strength, reaching into God for help, meaning this: 'Ah, Lord Jesus, king of bliss, how shall I have peace? who shall teach me and tell me what I need to know, if I cannot see it in you now?' Then our courteous Lord answered by showing, very mistily, a wonderful example of a lord who has a servant. (Ch. 50)

That story of the Lord and the Servant brought me once more to the gates of Eden.

CHAPTER FOUR

The Dark Forest

THE VIEW from the gates of Eden, when I arrived, was not an encouraging one. God had turned Adam and Eve out of Eden and posted cherubim with flaming swords to guard the gate against them. I remembered how Milton describes their departure in the last lines of 'Paradise Lost':

> They, looking back, all the eastern side beheld
> Of Paradise, so late their happy seat
> Waved over by that flaming brand; the gate
> With dreadful faces thronged, and fiery arms.
> Some natural tears they dropped, but wiped them soon;
> The world was all before them, where to choose
> Their place of rest, and Providence their guide.
> They, hand in hand, with wandering steps and slow
> Through Eden took their solitary way

But I had to bear in mind that this is not the end of the story. 'Paradise Lost' is only the first instalment of a two-part story. It has a sequel with a happy ending – 'Paradise Regained'. The happy ending is not quite, as in the best fairy stories, 'and so they all lived happily ever after' – but it is close to it. The story ends 'and so they were all *able* to live happily ever after'. For God does not leave Adam and Eve in exile. He sends his own son as a second Adam to redeem the first Adam's fall.

I thought I had better read what St Paul said about this when he wrote to the Christians in Rome about twenty-five years after the crucifixion:

> Sin entered the world through one man, and – through sin – death, and thus death has spread through the whole human race, because everyone has sinned.... Adam prefigured the One to come, but the gift itself considerably outweighed the Fall. If it is certain that through one man's fall so many died, it is even more certain that divine grace, coming through the one man Jesus Christ, came to so many as an abundant free gift.
>
> The results of the free gift also outweigh the results of one man's sin. For after one single fall came judgement with a verdict of condemnation. Now after many falls, grace comes with a verdict of acquittal.
>
> If it is certain that death reigned over everyone as a consequence of one man's fall, it is even more certain that one man, Jesus Christ, will cause everyone to reign in life who receives the free gift, which he does not deserve, of being made righteous.
>
> Again, as one man's fall brought condemnation on everyone, so the good act of one man brings everyone to life and makes them justified. As by one man's disobedience many were made sinners, so by one man's obedience many will be made righteous. When the law came, it was to multiply opportunities for falling – but however great the number of sins committed, grace was even greater. And so, just as sin reigned wherever there was death, so grace will reign to bring eternal life – thanks to the righteousness that comes through our Lord Jesus Christ. (Romans 5: 12, 15–21)

So the story that started out looking like a tragedy has a happy ending. It sounded such a happy ending, in fact, that I was surprised it needed a second light on it. But a second light – or rather a second sight – is just what I found Julian brings, with her stereoscopic vision that 'sees two different pictures at once and sees all the better for that'. But before I set out to explore her new view of the Fall, I realised with some foreboding I must first hack my way through the forest of Original Sin.

It is a forest that casts a long shadow. I remembered an occasion when I had been cooing over a new baby in company with its grandmother – something I seem to do with increasing frequency since I have become a grandmother myself – when she had suddenly burst out: 'Isn't it terrible of the Church to talk about Original Sin, and to say that this darling little baby is born wicked!' At the time, all I could think of to say was: 'I don't think it's like that, exactly.'

For it seemed to me that the doctrine of Original Sin is not that all of us are born wicked. The doctrine of Original Sin starts, surely, from the fact that once all of us were good. Belief in Original Sin depends first on believing in original virtue.

Adam and Eve were created in God's image, and they were forbidden to eat the fruit of the tree of knowledge of good and evil. But it was not because God wanted to build some sort of booby trap into Eden – just so that he could have the satisfaction of seeing them fall into it. They were forbidden to eat it because, for mankind, the knowledge of good and evil does bring death.

The serpent told Eve: 'You will not die. God knows in fact that on the day you eat this fruit your eyes will be opened and you will be like gods, knowing good and evil.' He lied – as serpents do.

When they ate the fruit, Adam and Eve did indeed know good and evil – but they did not become as gods. For gods can know evil by pure intelligence, without being involved in it. But for mankind, the only way to know evil is by experiencing it.

So the doctrine of Original Sin does not mean that the baby comes into the world as a born cheat and liar. It means the baby comes into a world where it will know every kind of evil – and not be protected from knowledge of it.

This is Adam's legacy to us – the fact that we shall suffer the experience of evil whether we choose to or not. We inherit the results of Original Sin, even though we were not the original sinners. 'By one man's disobedience many were made sinners,' St Paul wrote.

Julian believed all this. Her dilemma was that she was asked to believe something extra. On the one hand, the teaching of the Church told her that Adam sinned, and that we sin in our turn – and so we deserve blame and judgement. On the other hand, God showed her that he did not blame us for our sin.

God judges us by our true inner nature, which is always kept whole in him, safe and sound forever. And this judgement comes from his rightfulness. But men judge us by our outward, changeable, nature. This seems now one thing, now another, as it runs after first this and then that. And all this shows outwardly. . . . The first judgement, which springs from God's rightfulness – that is, of his high endless love – is the good and lovely judgement that I saw in all the wonderful revelations, where I saw him assign no whit of blame to us.

But although this was sweet and lovely, yet I could not be fully at peace simply by looking on it. And this was because of the judgement of holy church, which I had learnt beforehand, and which was always in my mind.

Because of the church's judgement, I understood that I must recognise myself as a sinner – and I also understood, by the same judgement, that sinners sometimes deserve anger or blame in God. And because of this I had a longing that was greater than I am either able or allowed to tell.

For God himself showed me the higher judgement at that time – and therefore I must needs accept it. And the lower judgement was taught me by holy church – and therefore there was no way in which I could forsake the lower judgement.

And to all this I had no direct answer, but simply wonderful example of a lord and a servant. And I still stand in longing, and shall until I die, to understand – by grace – the two judgements as I ought to. (Ch. 45)

I realised that if I was going to try to traverse the forest of Original Sin by the light of Julian's lantern I must – as she did – go slowly, and pick my way carefully. This is how her story of the Lord and the Servant begins:

I saw two actual people, that is to say, a lord and a servant. And God let me understand them spiritually.

The lord sits with dignity, at rest and in peace. The servant stands reverently by before his lord, ready to do his will. The lord looks upon his servant lovingly and tenderly, and gently sends him to a certain place to do his bidding.

The servant does not simply go, but leaps up and runs off at great speed to do his bidding, because he loves his lord. And then he falls into a gully and is very badly hurt. And then he groans and moans, and wails and writhes, but he cannot get up or help himself at all.

And in all this, the worst thing I saw befall him was that he had no comfort. For he could not turn his head to look upon his loving lord, who was near him and from whom all comfort flows. But, like a man who for a while is weak and foolish, he gave himself up to grief and languished in sorrow, and in this sorrow endured seven pains.

The first is the great bruises he got in his fall, which caused him great pain. The second was the lethargy of his body. The third was the weakness that came from these two. The fourth, that he was so blinded in his reason and stunned in his mind that he had almost forgotten his love of doing his lord's will. The fifth was that he could not get up. The sixth astonished me most, and that was that he was all alone. I looked all around, far and near, high and low, and saw that there was no one to help him. The seventh was that the place where he lay was narrow, hard and harsh. I wondered how this servant could suffer all this pain so uncomplainingly.

And I looked carefully to see any blame or fault in him, or if his lord should lay any blame on him, and truly, there was none to be seen. For the only reason he fell was because of his good will and his great desire – and he was still as eager and good at heart after he fell as he was when he stood before his lord, ready to do his bidding.

And even so, his loving lord looked upon him tenderly, and this time with a double regard. One – outward – look was gentle and kind with great tenderness and pity. And this was the first level of the Showing. The other level was inward and more spiritual, and this was shown by leading my understanding into the lord. In this, I saw him rejoicing greatly because of the great rest and glory he will bring his servant by his abundant grace. This was the second level of the Showing, and then my understanding was led back into the first, keeping both in mind. (Ch. 51)

I thought I had better start by comparing this with the Genesis story. I could see at least three things that are different. First – the servant, who is Adam, wanted to please God, not to disobey him, when he fell: 'For the only reason he fell was because of his good will and his great desire.' So the Fall is an accident, not a deliberate act of wrong-doing.

Second – even when he had fallen, Adam did not become sinful: 'He was still as eager and good at heart after he fell as he was when he stood before his lord, ready to do his bidding.'

Third – God is not angry with Adam: 'One look was gentle and kind with great tenderness and pity.' Indeed God, far from condemning Adam, actually rejoices in man's Fall: 'I saw him rejoicing greatly because of the great rest and glory he will bring his servant by his abundant grace.'

It was beginning to be clear to me that the picture that Julian's 'second eye' was being shown is a post-incarnation view of the Fall – the Garden of Eden seen from the vantage point of Calvary. God's purpose in allowing the serpent into Eden is beginning to come into focus.

The temptation was not, as I had already realised, a booby trap – nor was it some kind of initiative test that Adam failed. Nor was it a terrible accident that God had not foreseen. God himself had made the serpent, after all, on the sixth day, and knew perfectly well that he was slithering round Eden. The Fall was permitted because it was only by allowing Adam to know evil that God could enable him fully to know good. But God did not force him to know evil. Adam himself had to make the choice.

> Then the courteous Lord said this: 'Behold my much-loved servant, what harm and hurt has he got in my service for love of me – yes, and all because of his good-will. Is it not right and proper that I should repay him for his fear and his fright, his hurt and his harm, and all his sorrow? And, more than this, does it not fall to me to give him a gift that is better and more honour to him than his own lack of harm would have been? It seems to me I should do him no favour if I did less.'
>
> And from this, an inward spiritual understanding of the Lord's meaning sank into my soul. By this I saw that it surely must be – by the very fact of his greatness and glory – that

the lord would reward his servant he loved so much – and would reward him truly, blessedly and without end – far more than he would have done if the servant had not fallen. Yes, and reward him so lavishly that his fall, and the harm he got from it, are all turned into high, unimaginable glory and everlasting joy. (Ch. 51)

This, I realised, is the core of the truth Julian was given to understand again and again in the Showings: – that, improbable as it sounds – good cannot be fully known without knowing evil; that sin is the gate to glory; that it is the nature of the power of God to bring good out of evil; and that it is the essence of the nature of evil that it can become the raw material of good.

This astonishing fact is built into Julian's most often quoted words 'All shall be well'. But the words are God's, not hers, and the first time God speaks them they are prefaced by 'Sin is behovely'. When I was translating Julian's book, I found 'behovely' was untranslatable and so glossed it as 'it had to be' and kept the original alongside it so the whole passage read: Sin is behovely – it had to be – but all shall be well, and all shall be well, and all manner of thing shall be well.

I knew, of course, that Julian wasn't the first or the only one to find this out. Some of St Paul's best-known words come from his letter to the Romans: 'Where sin abounded, grace did much more abound . . . Shall we continue in sin, that grace may abound? God forbid!' But it seemed to me that the centuries before our own, with their belief in the Fall of Man, could appreciate the connection between sin and grace. Our own age, with its belief in the Rights of Man, has lost sight of it. I recalled that wonderful carol from Julian's day:

Adam lay y-bounden
Bounden in a bond

Four thousand winters
Thought he not too long

And all was for an apple
An apple that he took
As clerkes finden
Written in their book

Ne had the apple
The apple taken been
Ne never had our Lady
A-been heavene queen

Blessed be the time
That apple taken was
Therefore maun we sing
Deo Gratias.

The people in Julian's day believed the Bible stories were literally true, and they knew them inside out. They painted them on the walls of their churches, they carved them in bosses, they acted them in their mystery plays. Some mystery plays were already being performed in the streets of Norwich when Julian was a girl, and by the end of her life it's probable that the complete cycle of the famous Norwich plays was being performed every year. Certainly the York cycle was, because Margery Kempe saw it – and there's every reason to suppose that Norwich, the second city in England, would have been a jump ahead. The first scene of the play cycle was always the story of the Fall – and the whole audience knew perfectly well that there was a happy ending.

So why, I wondered, did Julian need to be shown a 'second sight' of the Fall? At first it looked to me as if she was saying the same thing as St Paul when she writes:

And to this our blessed Lord answered with a most kind look and showed that Adam's sin was the worst harm that was done and ever shall be until the world's end. He also showed that this is clearly known by all Holy Church on earth. More than this, he taught me I should look upon the glorious Atonement. For this making amends is more helpful to the salvation of many, without compare, than ever the sin of Adam was harmful.

What our Lord means by this teaching is that we should remember this: 'Since I have brought good out of the worst evil, I want you to know, by this, that I shall bring good out of all lesser evils, too. (Ch. 29)

Then I looked at St Paul's words again:

The results of the free gift also outweigh the results of one man's sin. For after one single fall came judgement with a verdict of *condemnation*. Now after many falls, grace comes with a verdict of acquittal . . . Again, as one man's fall brought *condemnation* on everyone, so the good act of one man brings everyone to life and makes them justified. As by one man's disobedience many were made sinners, so by one man's obedience many will be made righteous.

I saw they parted company in the word 'condemnation'. St Paul sees that 'one man's fall brought *condemnation*'. Julian is shown that God does not blame us for our fall. She writes:

His will was kept whole in God's sight. For I saw our Lord commend and approve his will, even though the man himself was held back, and was so blinded that he did not know what his own will was. (Ch. 51)

Julian's view of the conflict is not, like St Paul's, a battle between equal forces, but a confused scuffle in the dark.

All of us who shall be saved have, during this lifetime, an amazing mixture of good and ill within us. We have within us Jesus, our risen Lord. We have within us the misery of the mischief of Adam's fall and dying. By Christ we are steadfastly kept safe, and by his touch of grace we are lifted up to sure hope of salvation. By Adam's fall we are so fragmented in our feelings in so many ways – by sins, and sundry pains – that we are in the dark, and so blind that we can scarcely know any comfort.

But in our inward will we wait upon God and faithfully trust to have mercy and grace. And this is his own work in us. And in his goodness he opens the eye of our understanding and gives us sight – sometimes more and sometimes less, as God makes us able to understand it. And now we are lifted up to one, and now we are allowed to fall into the other.

And this is such an amazing mixture in us that we scarcely know how we or our fellow-Christians stand because of these astonishing mixed feelings. But the same holy will, which we give to God when we perceive him, is always truly willing to be with him – with all our heart and strength. And so then we hate and despise our evil promptings and everything that could be the occasion for sin – both spiritual and bodily.

But this then is our comfort: that we know in our faith, by virtue of Jesus who safeguards us, that we never give our will to them. But we rail against them, enduring pain and sorrow, and praying, until the time comes when he shows himself to us once again. And so we live in these mixed feelings all the days of our life. (Ch. 52)

I saw there was no doubt, in Julian's account, about the outcome of the battle. We are at a disadvantage because Adam's Fall has confused and blinded us, but the Fall has not made us into born losers. For even though we lose sight of God, Julian is assured that he does not lose sight of us. We shall not be overcome, because God himself is within us, built into our nature – and we have a 'godly will' within us.

In these Showings I saw and understood that in every soul that shall be saved there is a godly will that never assented to sin, nor ever shall. This will is so good that it can never will any evil. But always and forever it wills good, and does good, in the sight of God.

And then, unexpectedly, after I had condemned St Paul for his message of condemnation, it just so happened (and Julian says 'nothing happens by chance') that the day's epistle was part of his letter to the Hebrews. I found him quoting Jeremiah (31: 31–4), and discovered that both Paul and Jeremiah seemed to be saying exactly the same thing as Julian. St Paul writes:

By virtue of that one single offering, Christ has achieved the eternal perfection of all whom he is sanctifying. The Holy Spirit assures us of this; for he says, first:

This is the covenant I will make with them when those days arrive; and the Lord goes on to say:

I will put my laws into their hearts and write them on their minds. I will never call their sins to mind, or their offences. (Hebrews 10: 14–17)

Surely, it seemed to me, *'never call their sins to mind'* means that God puts no blame upon us, and *'I will put my laws into their hearts and write them on their minds'* is identical to Julian's perception of our 'godly will'. The difference between them is that the message Julian was given is a message which carries the implications of this covenant to their logical – and astounding – conclusion:

And our Lord wills that we know this in our Faith and Belief – specifically and truly – that we all have this godly will, entire

35

and safe, in our Lord Jesus Christ. For, because of God's right-fulness, the same human nature that shall reach fulfilment in heaven needs must be so knitted and joined to Christ that there is a substance within it that never can, nor ever shall, be separated from him. And it is through his own goodwill and his endless farsighted purpose that this is so.

And I saw that it is his will that we know that he does not take the Fall of any one of those who shall be saved any harder than he took the Fall of Adam. And we know that he loved Adam endlessly, and looked after him safely in his needs – and that now he has blessedly restored him in high unimagin-able joys. (Ch. 53)

It seemed to me that, when people think about the Fall, they often lose sight of the fact that God 'loved Adam endlessly'. And as I struggled through the dark forest of Original Sin I realised that the light from Julian's lantern was kindled and fuelled by that endless love. For, of course, when Adam and Eve were turned out of Paradise, God's response was, not to bar the gate for ever, but to find a way to bring them back to their proper place. And so, as the gates of Paradise clanged shut behind Adam, I realised I had to push on further into the heart of Eden and try to understand what Julian's 'second eye' was shown about the coming of the second Adam to redeem the first Adam's Fall.

CHAPTER FIVE

Adam's Old Shirt

A S I PICKED my way slowly along the overgrown track, I realised that Julian, too, had encountered thickets that she had to struggle through. Among the most impenetrable was the fact that the servant in the Lord and Servant story stood for Christ as well as for Adam. (All quotations in the Lord and the Servant are from Ch. 51.) It took Julian more than twenty years to reach the end of that particular path. Her first idea is simply that the servant is the first Adam:

> The servant who stood before the Lord I understood was meant as Adam – that is to say, one man was shown then, and his fall, to make it plain from this how God regards a man and his fall. For in the sight of God all men are one man, and one man is all men.

But she realised that, though the story had been given her to answer her question of how God looks on us in our sin, this simple identification did not help her:

> But in spite of the prompting God gave me, the example still perplexed me. For I thought it had been given me to answer my questions (whether God blames us for our sin) and yet I could not understand it well enough to give me any comfort at that time. For, as I shall tell, I saw many properties in the

37

servant (who stood for Adam) that could not possibly belong to one man (Adam) alone.

Slowly Julian gropes her way towards an understanding. First she is shown many wholly unexpected properties that *do* belong to the first Adam. She is shown that, in some extraordinary way, when Adam was turned out, God himself was turned out, too. For God had made man's soul so that he could live in it, and so when mankind was homeless, God himself, in some way, became homeless, too.

> The place where the lord sat was simple, on barren earth, alone in the wilderness. His clothes were wide and flowing, as befits a lord. The colour of his clothes was blue as azure, sober and lovely. His look was merciful. The colour of his face was light brown, with handsome features. His eyes were black, beautiful and seemly, with a look of lovely pity. Within him was a great court, long and broad, all full of endless heavens.
>
> His sitting on the bare and desert earth is to mean this: he made man's soul to be his city and dwelling place, and man's soul is most pleasing to him of all his works. But while man had fallen into sorrow and pain, he was not fit to be his city. And so our own Father would not choose himself another place, but sits on the earth waiting for mankind, who was made from earth, until such time as his dear Son, with hard labour, has brought his city back to noble beauty again.

For Julian is shown that the very act of creation creates a need. By making mankind and separating them from himself, God somehow became less complete, and made a space that only man could fill – so that when Christ brought back mankind, through his Passion, he restored, not just man's loss of Paradise, but God's loss of man:

> Now the lord no longer sits on the bare earth in the wilderness, but he sits on the noblest throne that he has made in heaven

for his pleasure. Now the Son no longer stands before the Father in awe as a servant, poorly clad and half naked. But he stands directly in front of the Father with a crown of precious richness on his head. For it was shown that we are his crown – and that crown is the Father's joy, the Son's glory, the Holy spirit's delight and the endless wondering joy of all who are in heaven.

On top of this, Julian was shown that the servant had a job to do. Somehow, at the back of my mind, when I thought about Christ's coming as the second Adam, I had always had some sort of mental picture of the first Adam being lugged, helpless, from the jaws of hell. But Julian is shown that the Fall does not simply turn us into victims to be plucked from peril:

And inwardly, I was shown a fountain of love in [the servant]. And the love he had for his lord was just the same as the love his lord had for him. And the servant, in his wisdom, saw in his heart that there was just one thing which could be done to honour his lord. And the servant, for love (taking no thought for himself or what might befall him) quickly set off and ran at his lord's bidding to do the thing that was his lord's will – to do him honour . . .

There was a treasure in the earth which the lord loved. I marvelled and wondered what it could be. And I was answered in my mind: 'It is a food which is sweet and pleasant to the lord.' For I saw the lord sit as a man, and yet I saw neither meat nor drink that could be given him. This was one wonder. Another wonder was that this great lord had only one servant, and he sent him out on an errand. I looked at this, wondering what sort of work it might be that the servant had to do.

And then I understood he should undertake the greatest

labour and the hardest toil there is – he should be a gardener. He should dig and delve, toil and sweat, and turn the earth over and dig into the depths of it, and water the plants in season.

And he should carry on his work in this and make sweet streams flow, and noble and plentiful fruit to spring forth, which he could bring to his lord and give him for his delight. And he should never turn again until he had prepared this food perfectly, as he knew it pleased his lord. And then he would take this food, with the drink within it, and carry it with ceremony to his lord. And all this while the lord would sit in the same place, waiting for his servant he had sent out.

And I wondered where the servant came from. For I saw that the lord had within himself endless life, and all manner of goodness – except for the treasure that was in the earth, and that treasure sprang from the lord, out of the wonderful depths of his endless love. But it was not a glory to him until the servant had prepared it nobly, and brought it before him with his own hands.

The nature of this work that Adam the gardener was able to do, in spite of his Fall, is something that took Julian years to comprehend. I have tried for years to understand it too. I believe it to mean that the Fall gives us an opportunity to give something to God which was not ours to give while we were still innocents in Eden: that God's joy in us is made complete by the work we offer him: that he delights in St Paul's preaching, in Julian's writing, and in all the things we all of us try to do with the gifts he has given us. For it seems to me that, because of the Fall, our obedience to God's will for us is not simply negative but creative. For tasting the fruit of the forbidden tree means not just that we have knowledge of good and evil. It means that we are able to give goodness

back to God of our own free will – and not because, in our innocence, we have nothing else to offer.

There is no path that leads right into the heart of this mystery,
and Julian herself never penetrated the depths of it. 'But twenty
years after the Showing, all but three months, I was taught
inwardly, as I shall set down. In this misty example, three meanings
of the Showings are hidden very deep. But even so, I saw that all
the Showings are full of secret things.'

As she searches to reach a fuller understanding, she is told, 'You
must pay close heed to all the circumstances and details that
were shown in the example, even though it seems to you they were
obscure and unimportant.'

She observes the servant closely and describes him in detail:

> I saw the lord sit in state, and the servant standing reverently
> before his lord – not directly in front of him but partly to the
> side – the left side. He was dressed in a white shirt, just one
> garment, old and shabby, stained with the sweat of his body,
> narrow-fitting and short – about a hand's breadth below the
> knee – threadbare and looking as if it was nearly worn out,
> just about to fall into rags and tatters. And at this I wondered,
> thinking: 'These are most unseemly clothes for a servant who
> is so much loved to wear before so great a lord.'

The understanding that the servant is also Christ, the second
Adam, is not something she discovers for herself. It is given to her
suddenly. One moment she writes: 'And I did not understand what
this example meant – and this is why I wondered where the servant
came from.' Then, in a burst of illumination, she writes in the next
sentence: 'The servant stands for the Son, the second person of the
Trinity. And the servant also stands for Adam, that is to say, all
men.'

Having been given that insight, she then sets to work to
examine it:

41

The fact that the servant stands is a sign of work; to the side and on the left shows he is not worthy to stand directly in front of the lord. His setting off was the godhead, and the running was the manhood. For the godhead springs from the Father into the Virgin's womb, and falls to take our nature upon him. In this falling he took great hurt. The hurt that he took was our flesh, in which he had to bear the agony of the pains of death ... The fact that his shirt was just about to fall into rags and tatters shows the whips and lashes, the thorns and the nails, the pulling and the dragging, the tearing of his tender flesh ... And the twisting and the writhing, the groaning and the moaning, shows that he might never rise in his strength again – from the time he had fallen into the virgin's womb – until his body was killed and dead, and he had yielded his soul into his Father's hands, together with the souls of all mankind he was sent to save.

Slowly Julian realises the implication of this complete identification of Christ with Adam:

When Adam fell, God's son fell. For the holy joining which was made in heaven means that God's son could not be separated from Adam, and by Adam I mean all men. Adam fell from life to death in the pit of this miserable world, and after that he fell into hell. God's son fell, with Adam, into the depths of the Virgin's womb – who was Adam's fairest daughter. And he did it to take away Adam's blame, both in heaven and on earth – and with great power he fetched him back from hell. And by this our good Lord Jesus has taken all our blame upon him – and therefore the Father neither can, not wants to, put any more blame upon us than upon his own Son, beloved Christ.

And so Christ was the servant before he came into the

world, standing waiting before the Father, at his command, until the time God willed to send him out to do that glorious Deed by which mankind was brought back again to heaven.

And then he set off eagerly at his Father's command, taking no thought for himself and his great pain, and at once he fell low into the depths of the Virgin's womb. The white shirt is the flesh, that he had just one garment shows there is nothing between godhead and manhood; the narrowness is poverty; the age comes from Adam's wearing it; the sweat stains are from Adam's labour; the shortness shows the servant's hard work.

And so I saw the Son standing there, saying in his heart: 'Lo, my dear Father. I stand before you in Adam's shirt, all ready to set off and run. I will gladly be on earth to work to your glory when it is your will to send me. How long shall I wait in longing?'

For the result of the Fall was not, as the serpent promised, that men became 'like gods'. It was that God became man. For since it is true that, for man, the only way to know evil is by experiencing it, so Christ became man in order that God himself could know evil by experience – and no longer only by intelligence. But the experience of evil did not defile Christ. Julian sees that the experience of evil did not defile Adam, either. It could not, since when God created man, he did, indeed, make him in his own image. Here I realised that, in all my thinking up to now, I had seen the incarnation as a massive piece of condescension on the part of the Almighty. I believed that Christ accepted degradation when he took flesh, and that, after the resurrection, he was thankful to shrug it off and get back to being wholly God again.

But Julian perceives that 'Our nature was designed for him from the beginning: Christ has taken our lower nature upon him – and this nature was designed first of all for him.' (Ch. 57) 'It was God's endless purpose to make mankind. This fair human nature was first prepared for his own Son.' (Ch. 59)

If this is so, it means that the dark and thorny path through the forest of Original Sin leads directly to the gates of heaven. Far from being required to believe that we are all 'miserable sinners' and that 'this lovely little baby is born wicked' – we should be assured that our nature, open to sin though it is, is much nobler than we supposed. Julian's 'second sight' on the second Adam tells us that Christ was not demeaned by becoming man, but affirmed an indissoluble kinship.

She understands that the journey through pain and death that is the result of man's choosing to know evil is not punishment for sin, but the inevitable penalty of incarnation. It is a consequence, not a curse. The demonstration of this is that Christ himself, who was wholly sinless, nevertheless had to bear the consequence of sin. His willingness to bear it breaks the chain that links sin and blame: 'And by this our good Lord Jesus has taken all our blame upon him – and therefore the Father neither can, nor wants to, put any more blame upon us than upon his own Son, beloved Christ.'

Julian sees our whole nature is revealed to be – in essence – as glorious as Christ's in his incarnate manhood, and as pleasing and as blameless before the Father.

> And so he wills that we know that the noblest thing he ever made is mankind, and that the fullest substance and the highest virtue is the blessed soul of Christ. And, further, he wills that we know that Christ's dear soul was intricately knitted to him when he was made man. This knot is so subtle and so mighty that it is joined fast to God. And by this joining it is made forever holy. Furthermore he wills that we know all souls who shall be saved, in heaven without end, are joined by this joining and made holy by this holiness. (Ch. 53)

'Joined by this joining and made holy by this holiness' reminded
me of T. S. Eliot's 'Little Gidding', the last of his *Four Quartets* –
the poem in which many people have encountered Julian's most
famous words for the first time. And I realised that he, too, wrote
about a journey:

> We shall not cease from exploration
> And the end of all our exploring
> Will be to arrive where we started
> And know the place for the first time. . . .
> And all shall be well and
> All manner of thing shall be well. . . .

And so I saw that, on this leg of my journey, all my exploring
had brought me back to the Garden of Eden, where I started, and
I knew the place for the first time. The Fall was no longer a sentence
to a lifetime of guilt but a revelation of a love which outstrips our
understanding. Adam's curse had been transformed into God's
blessing:

> Blessed be the time
> That apple taken was
> Therefore maun we sing
> Deo Gratias.

CHAPTER SIX

Descend Lower

REFRESHING THOUGH it was to sit high above the world beside the transformed tree of knowledge of good and evil, I knew it was time to descend lower. For while one of the reasons people may be drawn to Julian is because her view of our original goodness is in cheering contrast to the view that we are all miserable sinners, I had to keep in sight the fact that, before sin can be transformed into good, it needs to be acknowledged and repented of.

And here I reached an obstacle blocking my path. Since the secular society no longer believes that sin exists, how could Julian's insight into the nature of sin provide the answer to my question 'why Julian now?' Surely if I explored this avenue I should be walking up a blind alley.

But at this point I decided that the way ahead lay, not on the well-trodden ground of proven fact, but in a detour through the undergrowth of supposition. I decided I had to work on the assumption that sin does exist – whether we go on believing in it or not. For it seemed to me that, if sin does go on existing, in spite of the fact that we believe it doesn't, Julian's view of the nature of sin would be precisely what is needed to cure the sickness caused by our own undiagnosed awareness-of-sin deficiency.

It was just this deficiency that Thomas Merton identified in *Conjectures of a Guilty Bystander* when he wrote that the New-

Found-Land was seen to offer the chance 'to escape from the burden of the past, to return to the source, to begin again a new history, starting off from scratch, without Original Sin'.

And Julian herself, though she would not have been able to imagine a world where people could think of themselves as sinless, perceives that the lack of awareness of sin can be a danger:

> But then, because of all this spiritual comfort that has been shown, a man or woman might be led, through folly, to say or think: 'If this is true, then it is good to sin so as to get a better reward', or else to think sin less sinful. Beware of this thinking. For truly if this thought comes, it is untrue and comes from the enemy of that true love that shows us all this comfort. (Ch. 40)

So while the main path of Julian's message leads to the understanding that sin can be transformed into great joy, and that the wounds of sin will be seen, not as scars, but as honours, I realised I could not get any further without nerving myself to turn aside and look upon sin that has not yet been transformed. It was such a difficult and discouraging expedition that I put off tackling it for years – and it comforted me to find that Julian herself was reluctant to tackle it, too.

> God brought into my mind that I should sin, and because of the joy I had in looking on him, I was reluctant to look on this Showing. But our Lord was patient with me, and gave me grace to listen. (Ch. 37)

Julian was never required to look on sin in the cold light that shows it as it really is:

> This is a princely friendship of our courteous Lord, that he tenderly protects us, even while we are in sin. He touches us secretly, and shows us our sin by the kindly light of mercy

47

and grace. (Ch 40). In his mercy, our Lord shows us our sin and our weakness by the kindly light of himself. For our sin is so vile and horrible that he, in his courtesy, will not show it to us except by the light of his mercy and grace. (Ch. 78)

Even so, the experience was still painful. But painful though it is, Julian was shown that – just as sin itself is 'behovely', necessary – it is also necessary to look on our sin and to acknowledge it. Because it is not until we have seen our sin, and recognised it, and repented of it, that the process of healing can begin:

But then repentance comes to them by the touch of the Holy Spirit, and turns their bitterness to hope for God's mercy. Then he begins to heal their wounds, and the soul begins to wake from death as it turns towards the life of holy church. (Ch. 38)

It is this dark place of recognition that I was so reluctant to enter. And the secular society, it seemed to me, can no longer get in. It has locked the door and thrown away the key. For the secular society claims that what the Church calls 'sin' is an arbitrary set of rules thought up by kill-joys to stop the rest of us doing what we want – that so-called 'sin', more often than not, is doing what comes naturally – whereas the Church requires us to put frustrating restrictions on our natural behaviour.

Julian's view is the opposite. For her, it is sin that is unnatural:

In this we can see that we have to hate sin by our very nature – and we have to hate sin by virtue of grace, too. And when, by God's help, we attune ourselves to nature and grace, we shall truly see that sin is, in truth, viler and more painful than hell – without compare – for it is against our fair nature. For as truly as sin is unclean, just as truly it is unnatural. (Ch. 63)

So I had to ask myself which view of human nature is right? Do we have a built-in pole of goodness to set our course by, or can we choose to strike out in any direction we please without doing violence to our nature?

It was while I was struggling to find the answer to these questions that I read the first chapter of Dorothy L. Sayers' *The Mind of the Maker* and these words jumped out at me:

> There is a universal moral *law*, as distinct from a moral *code*, which consists in certain statements of fact about the nature of man; and by behaving in conformity with which, man enjoys his true freedom ... The more closely the moral code agrees with the natural law, the more it makes for freedom in human behaviour; the more widely it departs from the natural law, the more it tends to enslave mankind and to produce catastrophes called 'judgements of God' ...
>
> Regulations about doing no murder and refraining from theft and adultery belong to the moral code and are based on certain opinions held by Christians in common about the value of human personality. Such 'laws' as these are not statements of fact, but rules of behaviour. Societies which do not share Christian opinion about human values are logically quite justified in repudiating the code based on that opinion.
>
> If however, Christian opinion turns out to be right about the facts of human nature, then the dissenting societies are exposing themselves to that judgement of catastrophe which awaits those who defy the natural law.

If this is true, it means that while we can move the goalposts of acceptable behaviour and can pass whatever laws we please to 'decriminalise' this or that, the further those laws diverge from the universal law that is built into our nature, the more we shall deviate from our course, and the more wretched we shall be. For the basis of crime and sin is not the same. Crime is defiance of a man-made set of rules that can be – and often are – changed. Sin is violating the unalterable law that is built into our nature. It follows that when we violate this natural law, the consequences are far greater that just that one act. It destroys the way we are meant to be. And that, in turn, destroys the whole fabric of our society. It becomes inevitable that things will go wrong – and the chilling words 'For he visits the sin of the fathers upon the children unto the third and fouth generation of them that hate him', are seen to be, not the petulant outburst of a capricious God, but a sober statement of the way things are.

The secular society has, logically, repudiated the code based on Christian opinion about the facts of human nature. There is surely a case for suspecting that, as a result, that society, where angry motorists kill each other, schools have to be protected by security fences, ninety-year-olds are robbed and raped, where patients attack their doctors and children their teachers, and where it is no longer safe to leave a toddler unattended for fear he will be abducted and murdered by other children – may be facing 'a judgement of catastrophe'. And if it is, it will not be because, in some simplistic way, God is angry with us, but because we have left something out right at the beginning of our calculation about human nature, which throws out the whole of the rest of the sum.

If the factor we have left out is sin, this could be the reason why Julian's insight into what sin is, is desperately needed. For if sin does violence to our nature, it is the sin itself that brings unhappiness – and it brings it in spite of the fact that it may be approved by society and whether or not it is condemned by the Church.

> Sin is the sharpest lash that any soul can be struck with. It is a lash that thrashes men and women and makes them loathsome in their own sight. (Ch. 39)

And Julian's perception that sin goes against our nature is bound up with a further insight into what our nature really is. She sees that we are all – in a way we can recognise but cannot explain – somehow interdependent and intricately linked together.

For if I look on myself alone, I am nothing. But when I think of myself and my fellow Christians joined together by love, I have hope. For in this joining lies the life of all who shall be saved. For God is all that is good, as I see it, and God has made all that is made, and God loves all that he has made. And he who loves his fellow Christians, for God's sake, loves all that is. (And he who loves thus, loves all.) For in mankind who shall be saved everything is included – that is to say, all that is made and the Maker of all. For in man is God, and God is in all. (Ch. 9)

And in Chapter 37 she writes:

What can make me love my fellow Christians more than to see that God loves all who shall be saved as if they were all one soul.

This underlying sense of in some way belonging to each other – whether or not we believe it is because we have our common origin in God – seems to me to be borne out by experience. It may be unlooked for, it may be unrecognised, it may be against all reason – but it is there. Sorrow and joy make us aware of it. Music, and art, and poetry – and the beauty of nature, too – assure us, by some mysterious process, that we are not random pieces of matter flung haphazardly into a meaningless universe, but part of a great company.

The journalist Martyn Harris, in *Something Understood* (*Daily Telegraph*, 25th May 1996) written to chart his struggle to come to terms with the meaning – if any – of life, in the face of his approaching death from cancer, wrote:

The *frisson* you get from a fine line of poetry comes chiefly, I think, from the sheer pleasure that someone has recorded something you thought only you had felt before. More than that, it comes from the realisation that many others have shared and will share this moment you had thought was unique and inexpressible. The loneliness of the individual life is dissolved briefly in a flicker of that same sensation of co-inherence.

The *frisson* is a shock, not of discovery, but of recognition – as when George Eliot wrote after reading Wordsworth (and surely no two people were more dissimilar): 'I never before found so many of my own thoughts so well expressed.'

This feeling, which brings an affirmation of one's inmost self, is quite different from the submerging of individual identity that unites a crowd swayed by mass emotion. Experiencing it does not depend on being part of a crowd, for it can be – usually is – found in solitude. It is a fellowship that leaps boundaries of time and space, so that a separation of a thousand years, and whole continents cannot conquer it: 'Read out my words at night, alone' wrote James Elroy Flecker in 'To a Poet a Thousand Years Hence' as he confidently addresses his 'friend unseen, unborn, unknown':

> Since I can never see your face
> And never shake you by the hand
> I send my soul through time and space
> To greet you. You will understand.

John Donne summed it up famously:

> No man is an island, entire of itself; every man is a piece of the Continent, a part of the main; if a clod be washed away by the sea, Europe is the less, as well as if a manor of thy friends or thine own were; any man's death diminishes me, because I am involved in mankind; and therefore never send to know for whom the bell tolls; it tolls for thee.

But the very beauty and familiarity of the words serves – it seems to me – to obscure the enormous implications of it. Martyn Harris writes it afresh for this century:

> And beneath that again, and deeper still, there seems to lie a recognition of connectedness and mutuality. I cannot function properly in society as an atom of pride and self-interest. I cannot survive in the universe as a chunk of matter randomly generated by impersonal physical laws. I have to hand myself over to the idea that I am reciprocally connected to other people and to the universe in ways I cannot understand and have humbly to accept. And that, in far too many words, is what I think I mean by love.

If it is true, the responsibility is inescapable. For if we really are interdependent parts of one creation, it follows that, if we behave as if we are unconnected individuals, whose conduct is of no concern to anyone but ourselves, then in some inexplicable way we damage and distort the natural pattern that binds us all together. This is not at all the same thing as feeling 'we are all guilty'. But it does mean we are all implicated. Implicated in what? What is sin? Julian's answer, as usual, is unexpected.

> I did not see sin. For I believe it has no substance or manner of being, but is only known by the pain it causes. (Ch. 27)

Whatever the cause, there is no lack of pain in our day. Our spiritual anguish seems to be increasing, in spite of the fact that the physical pains we have to put up with are far less and fewer than they were in Julian's day. Indeed, if the consumption of tranquillisers, the demand for counselling and the number of suicides is anything to go by, we seem to be more racked with psychological pain at the start of the twenty-first century than we have ever been before. Could the reason be that, in Julian's terms, we are 'sinning'? What are these 'sins' that lead us to act against our own nature?

Julian mentions only two sins specifically. Both of them are unexpected – and both of them, surely, there is reason to believe we suffer from today.

> God showed two kinds of sickness that we have; one is impatience and sloth, so that we make heavy weather of our toil and trouble. The other is despair and frightened fear. He showed sin generally, in which all evil is comprehended – but he showed only these two in particular. These two are the sins that most trouble and buffet us, as our Lord showed me – and he would have us cured of them. (Ch. 73)

'Impatience and sloth, despair and frightened fear' – these, surely, are not what we are accustomed to think of as sins. Of them all, only sloth figures on the list of the seven deadly sins – pride, anger, gluttony, avarice, lust, envy and sloth – and Julian transforms it by linking it with impatience, so that it becomes not idleness but, once more, lack of faith in God's goodness. For what these specific sins that Julian mentions have in common – which is the reason for their sinfulness – is that they have great power to cut us off from the sight of the God who loves us. This is what sin does.

And Julian's insight goes further. She perceives that, because no man is an island, other people's sins can cut us off from the sight of God just as effectively as our own:

> The soul that would remain in peace must, when another's sins come to mind, flee as from the pains of hell, searching into God for remedy against it. For looking on another man's sin makes, as it were, a thick mist before the eyes of the soul, so that for a time we cannot see the beauty of God – unless we look on those sins and repent with him, and have compassion on him, and pray to God for him. For unless we do this, another man's sin attacks, and batters, and hinders our soul. (Ch. 76)

If it is true, it seemed to me I had discovered yet another reason why Julian speaks so vividly to us today. Whether or not the sum of human wickedness is increasing is not at issue. What is certain is that never before have we been encouraged to look at it so often and in such detail. Other people's sins leap out at us every time we open a newspaper or switch on the television. Indeed, Julian might be writing to someone who has just watched the television news when she says:

> Something else I understood was this – that we see such evil deeds done, and such great harm caused by them, that it seems to us impossible that any good should come out of them. And we look on them, sorrowing and mourning over them, so that we cannot find rest in the joyful sight of God as we ought to. (Ch. 32)

And it seemed to me that Julian's insight that we should offer all this to God knowing that he can and will make all things well is desperately needed in our day. For, while on the one hand, the secular society badgers us with advice on what not to eat and drink in order to keep our mortal bodies healthy, no one seems to be aware of the damage that can be caused to our immortal souls by a constant diet of the junk food of other people's sins. They are set before us as our daily bread – and washed down by a spot of vintage Freud and diluted Marx. And they induce the soul-sickness that cuts us off from the sight of God and plunges us into hell.

But what, or where, is hell? Julian's concept of hell is as surprising as her concept of sin. For this hell is not the one she had been taught to believe in by the Church – the place of torment that awaits unrepentant sinners at the Last Judgement, a hell which was so vividly portrayed on every chancel arch in her day.

For Julian was shown that, because sin is unnatural, it creates its own hell – and is a place where sinners can find themselves here and now:

And in all this I asked, if I dared, to be given a clear sight of
hell and purgatory . . . But although I asked to see this, I saw
nothing at all. (Ch. 33). And I was shown no harder hell than
sin. For there is no hell but sin for a soul that is true to its
nature. (Ch. 40)

This understanding of hell is, surely, another reason why we
respond to Julian today. Hell-fire sermons no longer chill the blood,
and devils with pitchforks raise smiles rather than terror. But a
hell that cuts us off from our true nature, that blots out the sight
of God, and in turn alienates us both from ourselves and each
other is something we can recognise. A sense of alienation and
loss of identity is, surely, at the heart of our anguish at the start of
the twenty-first century.

For if sin really is going against the grain of our nature, it is
inevitable the sin itself will make us miserable. This is a reversal
of the view that our misery is of God's making – that he is pun-
ishing us for our sin – and perhaps even relishing the process.

Our courteous Lord does not want his servant to fall into
despair even when we fall into sin. For our falling does not
stop him loving us. For he looks on sin as sorrow and anguish
to those who love him and, because he loves them, does not
blame them for it. (Ch. 39)

And in the next chapter she writes:

And just as he does not stop loving us because of our sin, so
he wills that we should not stop loving ourselves or our fellow
Christians – but that we should nakedly hate sin, and love the
soul as God loves it.

Throughout her book, the key to Julian's understanding of sin
is that untranslatable word 'behovely'. For she was told over and
over again that sin, this built-in capacity for acting against our

nature, is behovely, necessary – it had to be. It is necessary because we can only grow to our full stature if we are exposed to it and reject it. It is necessary because it is only by experiencing sin that we suffer the pain it brings. And the pain itself is necessary – a part of the healing process:

> As for the pain, it is something, as I see it, that is timely, for it cleanses us, and makes us know ourselves and ask forgiveness. And because of our good Lord's tender love to all those who shall be saved, he quickly comforts them, saying: 'The cause of all this pain is sin. But all shall be well, and all shall be well, and all manner of thing shall be well.' These words were said so kindly, and without a hint of blame to me or to any who shall be saved. So how unjust would it be for me to blame God for allowing me to sin, when he does not blame me for falling into it. (Ch. 27)

And in the last few pages of the book she writes:

> Here our courteous Lord showed the weeping and wailing of the soul, meaning this: 'I know well that you want to live merrily and gladly because of my love, bearing all the penance that may come to you. But since you cannot live without sin, you have to suffer, for my love, all the sorrow, all the trouble, all the unhappiness that comes upon you. And this is so. But do not be too downcast by the sin that overcomes you against your will.' And here I understood that our Lord looks on his servant with pity, not with blame. For this passing life does not ask that we live completely without blame and sin. He loves us endlessly, and we sin continually, and he shows us our sin most tenderly. (Ch. 82)

This lack of blame which Julian shows us is, I believe, crucial to our understanding of how to deal with sin. For the bridge that stretches between sin and repentance is as narrow as a plank, with the hazards of a fall into despair on one side, and into indifference on the other:

> We should go at once to God in love. Not on the one hand crawling abjectly as if we were in despair, nor, on the other, being over-bold as if it did not matter. (Ch. 52)

For as we acknowledge the responsibility for our sin, at the same time we have humbly to acknowledge that God himself has accepted the overall responsibility, and has supplied the remedy:

> For he says: 'Do not accuse yourself too much, thinking that all your trouble and sorrow is all your own fault, for it is not my will that you should be overburdened with sorrow and misery.' (Ch. 77)

For Julian unerringly identifies the fact that the way we repent of sin can be a sin in itself:

> For when we begin to hate sin, and to mend our ways by the guidance of holy church, yet a fear still lingers and holds us back. This is because we see ourselves and the sins we have done before – and some of us see the sins we sin each day. For we do not keep our promises, nor the cleanness the Lord puts in us but fall into so much mischief that it is a shame to see. And looking on this makes us so sad and worried that we can scarcely find comfort. And sometimes we take this fear to be humility – but it is a wicked blindness and weakness. And we cannot scotch it as we do a sin we recognise, because it comes from the devil's work. And it is contrary to truth . . . For just as by this courtesy God forgives our sins when we repent – even so he wills that we should forgive our own sins of senseless worrying and frightened fear. (Ch. 73)

Of all the reasons why Julian speaks so directly to our troubled times, this insight, it seems to me, is one of the most compelling.

For although, if we are to understand our human nature fully, it is necessary to accept that sin exists, it is just as necessary that we should not impose a crushing burden of guilt on ourselves on account of it. Indeed the rejection of the concept of God by the secular society is surely a healthy reaction against this false notion of a God who first sets impossibly high standards and then punishes people for not achieving them.

So alongside our acceptance that sin exists must be Julian's steady vision of the fact that God looks on us with love. And to explore the depth of that love, I realised, with great foreboding, that I had to join Julian on Calvary at the crucifixion.

CHAPTER SEVEN

A Green Hill Far Away

THE IDEA OF standing beside Julian on Calvary horrified me. But I realised that, whereas the reluctance Julian and I had to look on sin had been the same for both of us, our reactions to looking at the crucifixion were completely opposite. So I had to ask myself why it was that Julian had a burning desire to understand the crucifixion as though she had actually been there, and why I was so disinclined to do anything of the sort.

As I considered this, I also realised that, whenever I had been speaking about Julian, I had always felt it necessary to preface the talk by explaining that her wish to experience the crucifixion as though she had actually been there was part of the accepted practice of meditative prayer in her day, and did not mean she was unbalanced, or neurotic, or masochistic. But always both my audience and I had felt – it seemed to me – that being present at the crucifixion was the last thing any normal person could possibly want. Yet Julian wanted it passionately:

> I wished I had been there with Mary Magdalen, and those others who were Christ's friends. And so I asked for an actual sight – through which I should have more understanding of the compassion of our Lady and all his friends who saw his agony and pain at that time. For I wanted to be one of them and suffer with him. (Ch. 2)

Without admitting it, I had always felt she must have been a glutton for punishment to want anything of the kind – and that only a spiritual giant could benefit from such an agonising experience. For I regarded my own Good Friday experience as a mortifying once-a-year penance that had to be undertaken solely in order to rejoice properly in the resurrection. And Julian's vivid images of Christ's suffering, which had leaped out at me from the pages of her book, made it seem likely that her view of the crucifixion would bring an even greater distress and sense of shame at the suffering I had caused.

> For that day when our Lord and blessed Saviour died upon the cross, there was a dry, frosty wind, as I saw it. And when all the precious blood that could, had bled out of his dear body, yet there was still moisture in his dead flesh, as I was shown. Loss of blood and pain dried it from within, and wind and cold dried it from without, and both met together in Christ's body. And although the pain of it was sharp and bitter, it was also long drawn out, as I saw it, and agonisingly dried out all the living essence of Christ's flesh. (Ch. 16)
>
> The blessed body hung alone there and dried for a long time, and the nails wrenched it as the weight of the body pulled against them. For I understood that, because of the softness of the tender hands and feet, the huge hard hurtful nails pulled the wounds wide open. And there was piercing and wrenching of the head, and the binding of the crown of thorns – all caked with dried blood with the sweet hair entwined with it – dried flesh sticking to the thorns and thorns to the dying flesh. (Ch. 17)

But when finally I forced myself to look steadily at what she writes about the crucifixion – rather than taking alarm at parts of it – I discovered a view that, although it was harrowing, was totally different from my own. I also found, uncomfortably, that I was forced to abandon the moral high ground of 'us' and 'them' I had hitherto occupied. Instead of loftily pointing out that the secular society had made a mess of things, I found I had to recognise that many believers – including me – had made a mess of things, too.

For it slowly dawned on me that a view of the crucifixion whose effect was to load believers with guilt and shame was just as spurious as the notion of a god who expected the impossible and then punished people for not achieving it. The secular society, it seemed to me, had shown better sense than the Church in rejecting both, even if it had thereafter lost its way in a moral wilderness. So here, it seemed, might be one more reason why Julian's book speaks so vividly today – and speaks to the Church, as well as to the world.

Bit by bit I recognised that my own attempts to come to the foot of the cross had, in fact, brought me no further than a hiding place on the edge of the crowds where, eyes shut and hands over my ears, I agonised over my responsibility for this tragedy Slowly I began to understand the motive of those few who stayed at the foot of the cross – a handful of women, among them his mother and Mary Magdalen – and St John – the only man strong enough to bear it.

For their motive in staying was not to heap blame upon themselves or to wallow in 'if onlys' – not to think over what they might have done to prevent the crucifixion, nor to acknowledge that their actions might have helped to bring it about. They came and stayed because they wanted to be there to share Christ's suffering – and so help him bear it. And Julian's motive was exactly the same:

> I willed that his pains should be my pains . . . [I asked] simply to suffer with him – as a loving soul might want to share with our Lord Jesus, who for love became a mortal man. (Ch. 3)

The confirmation that her motive is to join her suffering to Christ's, not indulge her own emotions, comes right at the start of the Showings. The priest who comes to give her the last rites holds the crucifix before her:

> At this, suddenly I saw the red blood trickle down from under the crown of thorns – hot and fresh and flooding out, as it did at the time of his Passion when the crown of thorns was pressed into his blessed head – he who was both God and man and who suffered for me. And I knew in my heart that he showed me this without any go-between. (Ch. 4)

The next words – before she is given any sight of the crucifixion – are these:

> And in this same Showing, suddenly the Trinity filled my heart full of joy.
>
> And I understood that this is how it will be in heaven without end for those who come there.

This joy comes right at the beginning, before anything else is shown her. The sight of the physical suffering will follow, and will cause her suffering she can scarcely bear, but through it all there will be the certainty that – at its deepest level – the crucifixion is a cause for joy.

Julian's experience of the crucifixion was not a simple re-enactment, but a many-layered perception: 'All this was shown in three ways: by outward sight, and by words formed in my mind, and by inward sight.' And as soon as, in her outward sight, she sees Christ's head begin to bleed, she is shown in her inward sight, not the crucifixion, but Our Lady. And she is shown her, not as she stood at the foot of the cross, but as she was before the annunciation:

> In my mind's eye I saw her as if she breathed – a simple,

humble girl, not much more than a child – the age she was when she conceived.

Then comes, in a few pages, the essence of the Showings, which she will expand and explore for the rest of her life: God's enfolding love and his care for the 'little thing the size of a hazel nut' – which is all creation; the insight that 'the goodness of God is the highest prayer that reaches right down to our lowest needs' and that 'the love that God most high has for our soul is so great that it outstrips our understanding'; and the recognition that 'Our inborn will is to have God, and the goodwill of God is to have us' (Chs 5/6). It is only after Julian has set down all this that she returns to the outward sight – the physical details of the crucifixion.

> While he showed what I have just set down to my inward sight, in my outward sight I saw Christ's head bleeding fast. The great drops of blood fell down from under the crown of thorns like pellets, as though they burst out of the veins. As it came out, it was brownish red, for the blood was very thick. As it spread, it became bright red, and when it reached the brows it vanished. Even so, the bleeding lasted long enough for me to see and understand many things.
>
> It was so lovely and lifelike that there is nothing to compare it with. It was as plentiful as the drops of water that fall from the eaves after a great shower of rain, that fall so thick and fast no one can count them. And for roundness, they were like the scales of herring as they spread on the forehead. This showing was vivid and lifelike, hideous and dreadful, sweet and lovely. And in all this sight it was enormous comfort to me that our God and Lord, who is so holy and mighty, is also so homely and courteous. And this filled me full of happiness and certainty of soul. (Ch. 7)

So, even at the same moment when she is first shown the sight of the crucified Christ, Julian knows comfort, and happiness, and certainty. Could those who stood on Calvary, I wondered, have felt like this? Surely for them the sight – as it had always been for me – would have been only 'hideous and dreadful' . . . 'sweet and lovely' would have had no part in it. And yet, I began to realise, 'hideous and dreadful' as being present at the crucifixion would have been, those words would not have summed up their whole experience. For just as Christ bore our grief and carried our sorrow, so they helped him bear his. The steadfastness that kept them at the foot of the cross brought about a transformation, so that they became, not grieving spectators, but participators. Julian recognised that because they joined their suffering to Christ's they became, through him, part of the whole sorrowing creation.

> Here I saw a part of the compassion of our Lady St Mary, for she and Christ were so joined in love that the greatness of his love caused the greatness of her grief. And so, in this, I saw the instinctive love, led on by grace, that all creation has for him. Here I saw a great communion between Christ and ourselves, as I see it, for when he was in pain, we were in pain. And all creation capable of feeling pain suffered with him. The firmament, the very earth itself, began to lose their nature with sorrow at the time of Christ's dying. For it is part of their nature to know and acknowledge him from whom their virtue springs as God. So when his strength left him, their strength left them too, in sympathy, as far as it could, in grief at his pain. And so those who were his friends suffered pain because they loved him. And all men in general – that is to say, even those who did not know – had to bear the loss of every kind of comfort, except for the deep, quiet keeping of God. (Chs 17–18)

I began to see, at long last, why the figures of Our Lady and St John are so often shown standing on either side of the cross. It was not simply that historically they were there. Their presence confirms that no man is an island – that grief and pain can be so borne that individual suffering is joined with Christ's suffering and, in turn, becomes a part in his salvation of the world.

Julian recognised that this pain leads to salvation even while she was enduring it:

> This showing of Christ's pain filled me full of pain, for though I knew well he suffered only once, yet it was his will to show it me and fill my mind with it, as I had often asked before. Then I thought: 'I little knew what pain it was I asked for', and like a fool regretted it, thinking that if I had known what it would be like I would not have prayed to suffer it. For I thought this pain was worse than death itself, my pain. I thought: 'Is any pain like this?' and I was answered in my mind: 'Hell is a different pain, for there, there is despair. But of all the pains that lead to salvation, this is the greatest – to see the one you love suffer.' (Ch. 17)

Julian chose to continue to bear these pains – for love of Christ, not in self-reproach – when she was given the opportunity to avoid them:

> Then I heard a word in my ear that said to me like a friend: 'Look up to heaven to his Father.' Then I saw clearly by faith that there was nothing between the cross and heaven that could have done me any harm. Either I had to look up or answer. I answered inwardly with all my soul's strength and said: 'No, I cannot, for you are my heaven.' This I said because I did not want to look away – for I had rather have borne that pain until the Day of Judgement than come to heaven by any other way than through him. So I was taught to choose Jesus as my heaven, though I saw him only in pain at that time.

And this has always been a comfort to me, that I chose Jesus as my heaven, by his grace, in this time of Passion and sorrow. (Ch. 19)

And she is given an insight that Christ's pain is not a lonely agony, but an agony of compassion:

And so I saw our Lord Jesus lingering on a long time – for the joining of godhead and manhood gave the manhood strength to suffer more for love than all men together could have borne. I do not mean only more pain than all those who shall be saved – from the first beginning to the last day – could tell, or count, or imagine – bearing in mind the worth of the highest glorious king and the shameful, despised and painful death. For he that is highest and most glorious was counted less than nothing and utterly despised. For the deepest truth of the Passion is to know and understand who he was that suffered.

For as much as he was pure and loving, even so much was he strong and able to suffer – for it was the sin of every man that shall be saved that he suffered for. And he saw the sorrow and desolation of every one of us, and grieved over it for love because he shared our nature. For as greatly as our Lady grieved over his pain, he grieved for her grief just as much – and more, because the manhood he bore was of even greater worth. And I, seeing all this through his grace, saw that the love he has for our soul is so strong that he sought our soul with great longing, and willingly suffered for it – and paid for it in full. (Ch. 20)

'Willingly suffered for it' is the key to the difference between the two opposing views of the crucifixion. Christ suffered for love – not under compulsion. Julian suffered with him for love – not out of guilt. And she is given resounding assurance of this when, having looked unflinchingly on the physical degradation of Christ's body on the cross, she thinks to see his death:

> Just at the same moment, it seemed, that I thought that life could last no longer and the sight of his end must be shown, suddenly, as I looked on that same cross, his expression changed to joy. This change in his blessed mood changed mine, and I was as glad and merry as can be. Then our Lord brought this gladly into my mind: 'Where is any part of your pain and grief now?' And I was overjoyed. (Chs 21–22)

For most of us, I suspect, whatever joy we find comes on Easter Day, not on Good Friday. Indeed, for most of my life, I came to realise, I had been behaving as though the crucifixion were, not a triumph, but a disaster. Never once had I caught a glimpse of the wonder of Christ's joyful obedience – his glad willingness to suffer. Never once had I seen the sight that Julian saw: 'Suddenly . . . his expression changed to joy'.

Realising this, I set out to discover what had blotted out the sight of this joyous love and replaced it with guilt and shame. I remembered that verse from 'Ah! Holy Jesus, how hast thou offended'. I found it was by J. Heerman (1585–1647) (was he Dutch or German, I wondered?) and has this verse:

> Who was the guilty? Who brought this upon thee?
> Alas, my treason, Jesus, hath undone thee.
> 'Twas I, Lord Jesus, I it was denied thee.
> I crucified thee.

I realised that I had come to recognise, through Julian, that it is a complete travesty of the truth of the crucifixion. We did not, could not, force God to suffer – could not drag him to the cross and nail him there against his will. It is our self-centred preoccupation with our own guilt that puts us in the starring role as criminals. It is the sin of pride that blinds us to the glorious fact of Christ's redeeming obedience – his tremendous 'let it be' – his over-whelming, generous and self-giving love. It is a spurious humility that makes our own hatred of ourselves more important than Christ's love for us.

Of course, the Church knows that the crucifixion is a triumph, not a disaster, but somehow it is a perpetual struggle to hang on to the awareness of it. For the Church must preach sin and repent-ance – and, as Julian saw, the very awareness of being sinful leads straight into another way of sinning – barren self-hatred and reproach. And she identifies this as the besetting sin of the Church:

> But because of the contradictions in us, we often fall into sin. Then this comes into our minds by our enemies' prompting, because of our own folly and blindness – for they say this: 'You know very well you are a fool, a sinner, and also unfaithful. For you do not keep the commandments. Often you promise our Lord that you will do better, and then straight away you fall in just the same way – particularly into sloth and wasting your time. For this is the beginning of sin, as I see it, especially for those who have given themselves to God to serve him by holding his blessed goodness in their hearts. And this makes us afraid to come before our courteous Lord. This, then, is how our enemy contrives to set us back with his false fears, because of our wretchedness and the pain he has in store for us. For he means to make us so worried and so weary by this that we lose from our minds the lovely, blessed sight of our everlasting friend. (Ch. 76)

In the fourteenth century they seemed to be more aware of the dangers of this particular form of self-reproach than we are today. The author of *The Cloud of Unknowing* echoes Julian's advice: 'Choose rather to be humbled by the unimaginable greatness and the incomparable goodness of God, than by your own wretchedness and imperfection. In other words, look more to God's worthiness than to your own worthlessness.'

The English Hymnal bears this out. There are some wonderful Passion hymns, but most are from Julian's day or earlier. With the nineteenth century the clouds of self-reproach begin to gather. One of the hymns by Mrs Alexander (1818–95) has this verse:

It was my pride and hardness
That hung him on the tree;
Those cruel nails, O saviour,
Were driven in by me.

And Mrs Alexander's contemporary F. W. Faber (1814–63) goes even further:

Ever when tempted let me see,
Beneath the olive's moon-pierced shade,
My God, alone, outstretched and bruised,
And bleeding on the earth he made.

And make me feel it was my sin,
As if no other sins there were,
That was to him who bears the world
A load that he could scarcely bear.

It is certainly a load that is too heavy for me to bear – and, through Julian, I have come to believe that God does not want me to. Our sin *is* vile and horrible, but it is 'so vile and horrible that God does not want our soul to be frightened by this ugly sight'. And this is why 'he shows us our sins by the kindly light of his mercy and grace', and why he wants us to know that 'just as he does not stop loving us because of our sin, so he wills that we should not stop loving ourselves or our fellow Christians'.

And what does Mrs Alexander's hymn 'There is a green hill far away' (my own childhood introduction to the crucifixion, incidentally – and many others' too, I would guess) tell us about the crucifixion?

> He died that we might be forgiven
> He died to make us good;
> That we might go at last to heaven
> Saved by his precious Blood. . . .

> O, dearly, dearly has he loved,
> And we must love him too.
> And trust in his redeeming Blood,
> And try his works to do.

The implication is clear. We are by nature wicked – Christ had to die in order to 'make us good'. If we had not been so sinful, this need never have happened. God, it seems, loved us then – not, it appears, loves us now – only because our sin had made it necessary, not because we are lovable. And his death lays on us the heavy burden of gratitude: 'dearly has he loved, and (so) we must love him too'. And ever afterwards we must make an heroic effort to pay off this unpayable debt 'and try his works to do'.

It is true that there was no other good enough to pay the price of sin, but I have come to believe that unless, like Julian, we look through the suffering to see the joy and love that made Christ pay it, the sight of that terrible price blinds us to the generosity of the giver. We fail to see the truth that, when Christ joyfully accepted crucifixion, he did it for love, to take away our sins – not to load us with a debt to burden us forever.

If it is true – as Brian Thorne claimed in his introduction to John Michael Mountney's *Sin Shall Be a Glory* (Darton, Longman and Todd, 1992) – that 'the ravages of the perverse messages of condem-

71

nation, inculcated by a guilt-inducing Church, have bitten deep into the collective unconscious of secularised men and women' – then surely this is why Julian's insight is urgently needed by the Church itself today, and not just by those outside it. For what can the Church give the despairing secular society if we have nothing to offer but a reflection of its own self-hatred? How can we heal them unless we first heal ourselves? If the Church is to tell good news – and not yet more bad news – it must be able to strip away the barren self-reproach and to perceive the deep truth that the crucifixion, as Julian was shown, is a triumph of love and a cause for rejoicing.

This change in his blessed mood changed mine, and I was as glad and merry as can be. Then our Lord brought this gladly into my mind: 'Where is any part of your pain and grief now?' And I was overjoyed. Then our good Lord Jesus said: 'Are you well paid by the way I suffered for you?' I said: 'Yes, Lord, I thank you. Yes, good lord, blessed be your name.'

Then said Jesus, our kind lord: 'If you are well paid, I am well paid, too. It is a joy, a happiness, an endless delight that ever I suffered my Passion for your sake. If I could have suffered more, I would have suffered more. . . .'

And I looked with great diligence to know how many times he would die if he could, and truly, the number was so far beyond my understanding that my mind had not the space or strength to comprehend it. And when he had died as many times as this, yet he would still think it nothing for love. For everything seems small to him when it is set beside his reward of love . . . For if he said he would make a new heaven and a new earth for love of me, this would deserve little reward, for he could do this every day if he wished, without any toil or trouble. But to die for love of me so many times that the number is too huge to reckon, this is the highest offer that our

Lord God can make for man's soul, as I see it . . . And here I saw that Christ's joy is complete, for his joy could not have been complete if there was any other way the work could have been done better. (Ch. 22)

Suddenly that green hill seems very far away. But Julian was able to reach this viewpoint only because she had first journeyed, for love, with Christ through all his pain and suffering. And on this journey she came to know that, not only is there deep joy in the depths of the crucifixion, but there is deep joy hidden in the depths of our own pain and suffering, too.

Thomas Merton wrote: 'We must see that the meaning of every man has been changed by the crucifixion; every man is Christ on the cross whether he realises it or not.' (*Conjectures of a Guilty Bystander*, p.219)

If we ask, as Julian did, to stand by him in his pain and sorrow, we find our role is transformed. No longer do we see ourselves as those who hammered in the nails – nor even as grieving bystanders:

> I understood that our Lord means that in his life we are on his cross with him in our pain and sorrow and our dying, and that if, of our own free will, we stay on that cross, with his help and grace, until the last moment, suddenly his expression will change and we shall be with him in heaven. (Ch. 21)

We discover the unimaginable truth that Christ does share his cross with us – in all its glory.

This poem by a hermit Sister puts the almost inexpressible into words:

> He does not send your pain
> but suffers it with you
> sharing in the bearing of it.

He does not send your pain
your grief is his grief.
He bore it first.
All the pain and all the grief
that ever was, or is, or will be
He has already borne on the cross.
Between you and the hard wood of your cross
hangs his crucified body
absorbing all your grief and pain.
'It is mine,' he says,
'I have paid to share in the bearing
of this very thing.'
He does not will your ill
but invites you to share
His cross.
This is not easy –
a cross that doesn't wound
is not a cross,
He does not will your ill,
His whole meaning is love.
So why – why is he letting this happen to you?
Well, why not?
He let it happen to Him –
all that injustice, grief and pain.
He could have called in
thousands of angels.
But he didn't. He let it be.
That's what crucifixion is –
letting it be.
That's what He is calling you to do –
'Let it be – in Me.'
We will never be asked to let it be
as He did

when the terrible 'forsaken' words
tore from his throat.
He alone took that medicine,
that ever afterwards
our 'let it be'
might be in Him – never forsaken.
Suffering passes
but to have suffered never passes.
Our wounds, placed
in the wounded hands
of the crucified One
are absorbed into his redemption of the world.
Suffering passes, but to have suffered never.
For to have companioned with him on his cross
transfigures our lives
and the lives of those around us
by the holy power of His redemptive love.

CHAPTER EIGHT

The Underground

W AS MY JOURNEY over, I wondered, once I had stood at the foot of the cross? What territory was left to explore? And it was then I realised that, in what Julian writes about sin and the crucifixion, there are two key passages which point to a tunnel that runs deep underground. The first is:

> But because of the contradictions in us, we often fall into sin. *Then this comes into our minds by our enemies' prompting*, because of our own folly and blindness – for they say this: 'You know very well you are a fool, a sinner, and also unfaithful. For you do not keep the commandments. Often you promise our Lord that you will do better, and then straight away you fall in just the same way – particularly into sloth and wasting your time.' For this is the beginning of sin, as I see it, especially for those who have given themselves to God to serve him by holding his blessed goodness in their hearts. And this makes us afraid to come before our courteous Lord. *This, then, is how our enemy contrives to set us back with his false fears, because of our wretchedness and the pain he has in store for us. For he means to make us so worried and so weary by this that we lose from our minds the lovely, blessed sight of our everlasting friend.* (Ch. 76)

And the second is:

For when we begin to hate sin and mend our ways by the guidance of holy church, yet a fear still lingers and holds us back. This is because we see ourselves and the sins we have done before – and some of us see the sins we sin each day. For we do not keep our promises, nor the cleanness the Lord puts in us but fall into so much mischief that it is a shame to see. And looking on this makes us so sad and worried that we can scarcely find comfort. And sometimes we take this fear to be humility – but it is a wicked blindness and weakness. *And we cannot scotch it as we do a sin we recognise, because it comes from the devil's work.* And it is contrary to truth. (Ch. 73)

How on earth, I wondered, was I supposed to follow this up? It was not just that the journey promised to be difficult or frightening. It was a tunnel so far removed from present-day thinking that, if I went along it, I felt I should be written off as a religious crank, and that anyone who had followed me this far would give up in disgust. I couldn't possibly – surely – be expected to go in pursuit of the devil in this day and age.

Yet I couldn't ignore it. Here, buried deep in what Julian says about sin and about the crucifixion were these two unmistakable references to 'our enemy'. Briefly I wondered whether to bank on the chance that no one else would notice those fatal words in italics and to skip quickly past the tunnel entrance on to safer ground. But in the end I realised unwillingly that, because I had undertaken to follow where Julian led, and not to stick to a course, I had no option but to dive in.

Julian first speaks of the devil early in her book, in the Fifth Showing, in Chapter 13:

And after this, before God spoke any word, he allowed me to look upon him for a while. And all I had seen and all the meaning of it was there, as far as the simplicity of my soul could understand it.

Then he, without words or opening his lips, formed these words in my soul: 'By this is the fiend overcome.' In this our Lord showed that it is his Passion that is the fiend's undoing. God showed that the fiend had the same malice now as he had before the incarnation. And, hard as he works, so he continually sees that all the souls of salvation escape him, gloriously, by virtue of Christ's Passion. And this is his sorrow, and he is put down, full of evil.

For all that God allows him to do turns to joy for us, and shame and woe to him. And he has as much pain when God gives him leave to work as when he is idle. And this is because he can never do as much evil as he would like, for his power is all taken into God's hands. But in God there is no anger, as I see it. For our good Lord always has in mind his own goodness and the rewarding of all those who shall be saved. He sets his might and his right in the path of the Evil One who, for wickedness and malice, busies himself to plot and work against God's will. Also, I saw our Lord scorn the devil's malice and expose his lack of power – and he wills that we should do so, too.

I began to wonder whether, just as there seemed to be an awareness-of-sin deficiency in the secular society, there might also be an awareness-of-the-devil deficiency that Julian's book is needed to correct. One great loss in throwing out the devil, it seemed to me, was that the blame for sin had nowhere to come home to roost but on mankind. Could this, I wondered, be another of the reasons behind our own sense of isolation and self-disgust?

For the truth of the matter, as Julian saw it, is that the Passion is necessary because of the devil's plotting, not because of man's wickedness. This is why God is not angry with man for his fall into sin, and does not blame him for it.

It's a neat answer, of course. If you don't want to blame man, or presuppose an angry god, the quick way out is to invent a scapegoat. Was 'the devil' a figment of our imagination, invented for just this purpose? What evidence could I find that the devil exists?

It just so happened that, when I was thinking about this, the gospel for the day was St Matthew 6: 7–15, which I read in the Jerusalem Bible translation.

> [Jesus said to his disciples:] In your prayers do not babble as the pagans do, for they think that by using many words they will make themselves heard. Do not be like them; your Father knows what you need before you ask him. So you should pray like this:
>
>> 'Our Father in heaven
>> may your name be held holy,
>> your kingdom come,
>> your will be done,
>> on earth as in heaven.
>> Give us today our daily bread.
>> And forgive us our debts,
>> As we have forgiven those who are in debt to us.
>> And do not put us to the test,
>> but save us from the evil one.'

There, embedded in the central prayer given by Christ to his Church, prayed every day by all Christians, was 'the evil one'. I could have no better authority than that. Feeling reassured, I set out to look more closely at what Julian has to say about the devil.

First I had to be aware that I was on a tightrope with a fall waiting on either side. I recalled what C.S. Lewis (an expert on 'the enemy') had written in his introduction to *The Screwtape Letters* (1942):

> There are two equal and opposite errors into which our race

can fall about devils. One is to disbelieve in their existence. The other is to believe, and to feel an excessive and unhealthy interest in them. They themselves are equally pleased by both errors.

And Screwtape himself (Letter VII) advises the young Wormwood:

> Our policy for the moment, is to conceal ourselves. Of course this has not always been so. We are really faced with a cruel dilemma. When the humans disbelieve in our existence we lose all the pleasing results of direct terrorism and we make no magicians. On the other hand, when they believe in us, we cannot make them materialists and sceptics ... I do not think you will have much difficulty in keeping the patient in the dark. The fact that 'devils' are predominantly comic figures in the modern imagination will help you. If any faint suspicion of your existence begins to arise in his mind, suggest to him a picture of something in red tights, and persuade him that since he cannot believe in that (it is an old text-book method of confusing them) he therefore cannot believe in you.

Judging by my own reaction, Screwtape and his friends have been extremely successful in the fifty-odd years since *The Screwtape Letters* was first published in blotting out the awareness of the devil in people's minds. And yet, looking back, I remembered that, when I first read Julian's book, it was a smooth-talking, worldly-wise devil who came unbidden into my mind.

The background was this. Back in 1972 I wrote a fighting article for the *Eastern Daily Press* opposing turning churches over to 'suitable secular uses'. This made me very popular with some people – and very unpopular with others, and a lot of them rang me either to agree or to attack me. But Alan Webster, who was Dean of Norwich, had a different reaction. He, too, rang me. 'Sheila,' he said, 'since you're so keen on prayer, I wonder if you would like to serve on a committee.' I was trapped and knew it.

The committee turned out to be one formed to organise the celebration of the 600th anniversary of Julian of Norwich – about whom I knew nothing. At the first meeting – to which I turned up wearing scarlet – I walked into a room full of black-clad nuns and clergy. I wondered how they could be so completely out of touch as to contemplate celebrating the anniversary of some obscure mediaeval nonentity.

After the meeting I read Julian's book. I ended up writing a one-act play[1] which begins with a dialogue between devil and archangel. Both are dressed as clergymen, the devil a resplendent trendy and the archangel a shabby parish priest. The devil voiced all my old thoughts. It starts like this:

> *Beelzebub*: My dear archangel, I must congratulate you. In my job as Devil Missioner, with special responsibility for making the Church look a fool whenever possible, I don't often get any help from your people. But your latest operation – this Julian woman – is an absolute gift.
>
> *Michael*: I know you well enough, Beelzebub, to know that you're going to tell me whether I ask you or not. What makes you think that telling people about Julian of Norwich is on the side of the devils?
>
> *Beelzebub*: But Michael, it's so quaint and dated! Here's this old biddy, I shall simply say, decently dead and buried nearly six hundred years, and the Church in this day and age has got nothing better to do than dig her up and make a song and dance about her.
>
> *Michael*: Do you really think the minds of men have been so far betrayed that they believe that nothing can be true unless it happened yesterday?

---

[1] *Mind Out of Time*, Julian Shrine Publications, 1979.

Beelzebub: I hope so! I've been working on it myself, and the playback I'm getting now is really very encouraging. I've been concentrating on change, change, change – which after all is what anyone with half an eye can see going on all around them – and I really think I've got it to the point where they assume that, because material conditions are different, then spiritual conditions must be different, too.

Michael: So your story is that Julian, simply because she lived in the thirteen hundreds instead of the nineteen hundreds, is automatically irrelevant.

Beelzebub: Carry on like that, and I'll have you converted, too. 'Irrelevant', a lovely word that, and very useful to us. I find it particularly handy when I set out to discredit everything, but everything, that was said, or done, or written, more than six months ago. It's only got one snag, and that's built into the system. Because I'm continuously discrediting past truths – even some of the ones I invented myself – I do get through an awful lot more material than I used to. [he sighs self-pityingly]

It seemed to me then, and still does, that there was and is great opposition to Julian's message being released into the world. But it is difficult to talk of the devil – and hard to keep one's eye on him. He slithers only briefly out of the leaves. And since he is essentially powerless, it is a mistake to elevate the battle between good and evil into an (almost) equal-but-opposite struggle, as Julian saw:

I saw our Lord scorn the devil's malice and expose his lack of power – and he wills that we should do so, too. Because of this sight I laughed aloud and made those who were round me laugh too, and their laughing rejoiced my heart. I wanted all my fellow-Christians to see what I saw, so they would all laugh with me. But I did not see Christ laugh, although I understood

82

that we may laugh aloud in comforting ourselves, and rejoicing in God because the devil is overcome.

And after this I became serious and said: 'I see three things – joy, scorn and truth. I see joy that the fiend is overcome. I see scorn because God scorns him and he shall be scorned hereafter. I see truth in that he is overcome by the blessed Passion and death of our Lord Jesus Christ, which was done in truth and with hard labour.

I thought of Judgement Day and of all those who shall be saved, whose happiness he greatly envies. For at that day he shall see that all the grief and trouble he has brought upon them shall be turned into even greater joy for them, without end. And all the pain and tribulation he wished upon them shall go with him to hell, without end also. (Ch. 13)

The battle between good and evil is already won. The devil is beaten, and the most he can do is to try to claw down human souls with him. And it was then that I realised for the first time that the devil is the missing element in the story of Lord and the Servant. It is, as I had worked out, Julian's 'second-eye' view of the story of the Fall. What had never struck me before was the fact that in this version the serpent is completely missing.

It cheered me up enormously to find that, even though Julian is so acutely – and to our eyes uncomfortably – aware of the devil, the plain fact is that when she was shown how God regards man and his fall, the devil's role was seen to be so insignificant that he is omitted from the cast-list altogether. Adam fell because the opportunity was there. He fell – he was not pushed. And the Fall itself was then used by God, not to punish Adam, but to reward him:

Behold my much-loved servant, what harm and what hurt has he got in my service for love of me – yes, and all because of his goodwill. Is it not right and proper that I should repay him for his fear and his fright, his hurt and his harm, and all his sorrow? And, more than this, does it not fall to me to give him a gift that is better and more honour to him than his own lack of harm would have been? It seems to me I should do him no favour if I did less. (Ch. 51)

The devil has served God's purpose – for if sin is 'behovely' – necessary – then it seems that the devil, though he did not realise it, was 'necessary' too. His own purpose has been completely overturned and the evil he intended has been turned to good. Having served his purpose he disappears from the scene and no longer even rates a mention.

In fact this disappearance is all that Julian is shown about damnation. When she asked to be given a clear sight of hell and purgatory:

I saw nothing at all – except as is set down earlier, where I saw the devil reproved of God and damned without end. I took this to mean all people who are in the devil's condition in life, and who die in that state. There is no more mention made of them in the sight of God and his holy ones than there is of the devil – notwithstanding they are of mankind and whether they have been christened or not. (Ch. 33)

But in spite of this, Julian did see the devil, though the only time he was able to appear was when she was asleep:

And in my sleep, I thought the devil clutched my throat – putting a face near mine like the face of a young man. It was long and very thin. I never saw one like it. The colour was red, like new-fired tiles, with black spots in it like freckles, darker than the tile. His hair was red as rust, cropped in front with long locks hanging at the side. He grinned at me with a sharp look, showing white teeth – which made it all the uglier. He had neither properly-shaped body nor hands, but held me by the throat with his paws, and would have strangled me – but he could not.

This ugly Showing came in my sleep, unlike all the rest. And in all this time I trusted to be saved and kept safely by the mercy of God. And our courteous Lord gave me grace to awake – and I was scarcely alive. Those who were with me saw this and bathed my forehead and my heart began to ease. Then a light smoke came through the door, with great heat and a foul stink. I said 'Benedicite Domine! Everything is on fire!' And I believed it was a real fire that would burn us all to death. I asked those who were with me if they smelt any smell, and they said no, they smelt nothing. (Ch. 66)

I wondered whether this would be enough to make people believe that Julian's experience was a delusion – and remembered the distinguished psychologist Robert Thouless's well-meant attempt, back in 1924, to explain away Julian's devil:

She lived the life of a celibate and solitary, so that neither her love for husband or children nor even her desire for human intercourse of a less intimate kind might distract her from an undivided love of God. But since the material from which her mysticism grew was human nature with instinctive desires craving their natural biological end, these suppressed elements in her mental make-up (particularly when weakened by illness) tended to break through their restraint and exhibit themselves in their simple and natural forms. These forms were to her evil because they were opposed to the super-natural redirection of her instinctive energies which was dominant in her character. Thus, primitive sexual desire remained a suppressed but not destroyed element in her psyche, and expressed itself in the vision of the young man who set him on her throat and thrust near her face a visage which was long and wondrous lean. The other elements – his

red hair, his paws and his malicious grin – may be regarded
as the reaction of her 'higher' nature against the primitive and
suppressed desires which were obtruding into her con-
sciousness.[1]

This laboured rationalisation quite failed to convince me that the
devil was a figment of Julian's imagination – particularly as I felt
sure that, far from having suppressed 'primitive sexual desires',
Julian had been married and a mother, widowed and bereaved.
Searching around for any evidence I could put forward that the
devil exists – and exists in fact, not as a manifestation of a dis-
ordered mind – I came to the conclusion that if I could, and without
taking what C.S. Lewis called 'an excessive and unhealthy interest'
in devils, I should put on record some small things that have
happened to me when speaking about Julian. The most usual is
that, directly afterwards, I am attacked by an overwhelming
feeling that I have made a complete fool of myself, I should never
have accepted the invitation in the first place, and that I should
never speak on Julian in public again. This is far more than any
natural dissatisfaction anyone might feel and could, if yielded to,
completely undermine all confidence in one's ability. By chance I
mentioned this to a friend who also speaks on Julian and found
his experience was identical. Out of interest I asked another friend
who speaks on Julian, and was told the same. Both are experienced
and talented speakers who had no ordinary reason to feel like this.
There are also other minor inconveniences – usually about travel
arrangements and computer discs (not least, I may say, while
writing this chapter). I perceive them as opposition, and sometimes
feel this may be a very small reflection of the attack Julian was
under herself.

For Julian's book has very great power to tell people of the love

---

1. *The Lady Julian*, SPCK, 1924, p. 63.

of God and, if there are demonic powers, must therefore arouse furious antagonism. If a minor speaker is troubled in this way, the opposition Julian must have encountered would have been formidable. Then I realised that this very same trick had been tried on Julian immediately after her Revelations in an attempt to undermine her confidence:

> For on the very same day that it was shown, when the sight of it had faded, I denied it like a fool, and openly said I had been raving. (Ch. 70)

It would have been a major victory for the forces of darkness if she had surrendered to this attack and her book had never been written.

But, formidable as it appears, the devil's power is illusory. Julian was shown that nothing can be done, either good or evil, unless God allows it:

> All that our Lord does is rightful, and all that he allows is praiseworthy. And in these two, both good and evil are included. Everything that is good is done by our Lord, and everything that is evil is done under his sufferance. I do not say that evil is praiseworthy, but that our Lord's allowing it is praiseworthy. In this his goodness shall be known for ever, by his loving-kindness and by the power of his mercy and grace. (Ch. 35)

And, because she was capable of undergoing it, Julian was tested to the very limit of her strength:

> And after this, the devil came back again with his heat and stink, and cost me dear – for the stench was so vile and painful, frightening and suffocating. Also I heard a noise, as if there were two people talking at once – holding a conference of great importance. And it was all a quiet muttering, and I could

87

not hear what they were saying. And all this was to lead me to despair, I thought – for it seemed to me they were mocking the prayers that are said loudly with the voice, but not with the devout intent and hard work that ought to be given to God in our prayers.

And our Lord gave me grace to trust him strongly, and to comfort my soul with spoken words – as I would have comforted someone else in trouble. And I thought that the effort it cost me was so great that it could not be compared with any physical strain. I set my eyes on the same cross that had comforted me before. I set my tongue to speak of Christ's Passion, and to say over the faith of holy church. I set my heart on God with all my trust and all my strength.

And I thought: 'You must make an enormous effort now, to stay in the faith, so that you are not taken by the enemy. If only you would make the same effort, from now on, to keep out of sin, it would be a good and sovereign occupation.' For I thought, truly, that if I were safe from sin, then I was surely safe from all the fiends of hell and enemies of my soul. And so the devil kept me busy all that night and on into the morning until it was about first light. And then they were all gone, all passed, and nothing left behind but the smell – and that still lingered awhile. And I scorned him. And so I was delivered from them by virtue of Christ's Passion. For by this is the fiend overcome, as our Lord Jesus Christ said before. (Ch. 69)

But it is just this battle with the devil that strengthens Julian's faith. If her plight had not been so perilous she would not have prayed so fervently – and so would not have been given so much grace. And although the outcome was not guaranteed – it would not be a battle if it were – she came to recognise that, hideous though his power seems at the time, the devil can do nothing

unless God allows it. And the reason for allowing it becomes clear
– it is so that God can reward us because of it.

It is by his permission that we are tested in the Faith and
made strong. For if our faith had no enemies it would deserve
no reward, as I understand our Lord's meaning. (Ch. 70)

The devil, too, is rewarded:

Our Lord showed me the enmity of the devil, by which I
understood that everything that fights against love and peace
– it is the devil and his crew. And because of our weakness
and folly we have to fall, but because of the mercy and grace
of the Holy Spirit we shall rise to even greater joy. And if our
enemy gains anything from us by our falling – for this is what
pleases him – he loses much more by our rising through love
and humbleness. (Ch. 77)

And, hard as he works, so he continually sees that all the
souls of salvation escape him, gloriously, by virtue of Christ's
Passion, and he is put down, full of evil. (Ch. 13)

The enmity of the devil – of forces of evil that fight against us –
is, I believe, actual and is recognised by most Christians. St Paul,
in his letter to the Ephesians, writes:

Put on all the armour which God provides, so that you may
be able to stand firm against the devices of the devil. For our
fight is not against human foes, but against cosmic powers,
against the authorities and potentates of this dark world,
against the superhuman forces of evil in the heavens. Therefore, take up God's armour; then you will be able to stand
your ground when things are at their worst, to complete every
task and still to stand. Stand firm, I say. Fasten on the belt of
truth; for coat of mail put on integrity; let the shoes on your
feet be the gospel of peace, to give you firm footing; and, with

all these, take up the great shield of faith, with which you will be able to quench the flaming arrows of the evil one. Take salvation for helmet; for sword, take that which the Spirit gives you – the words that come from God. (NEB, Ephesians 6: 12–17)

Unless we recognise there is a fight on our hands, we go naked on to the battlefield. And if Julian's book serves to tear away the cloak of invisibility the devil has cast round himself, then this is one more compelling reason why it is so much needed in our day.

CHAPTER NINE

The Battlefield

A S I LEFT the battlefield, I realised that Julian's shield – and her weapon – in her fight with the devil was prayer:

> I set my eyes on the same cross that had comforted me before. I set my tongue to speak of Christ's Passion and to say over the faith of holy church. I set my heart on God with all my trust and all my strength. And I thought 'You must make an enormous effort now, to stay in the faith, so that you are not taken by the enemy' . . . I thought that the effort it cost me was so great that it could not be compared with any physical strain. (Ch. 69)

I wondered whether I could find any link between this and the reason why her book is so much needed today. She prayed – like most of us do – out of dire necessity. Knowing she was in danger, she clung to prayer like a drowning man to driftwood.

For danger drives us all to pray. The most convinced atheist in the world finds himself crying 'God help me!' as the ship sinks. I thought perhaps there was a parallel in our day in that, after some dreadful tragedy, the victim's church is always packed with people who never normally come there. They come with a deep need to pray. They come to pray for peace for the souls of those who have died, for comfort for those who mourn, for (one hopes) forgiveness for those responsible, and for courage for the survivors – and the whole community – to face the future. But above all, I suspect, they come because they feel the threat and danger of the presence of evil and know that prayer can and does make sense of the apparently senseless, and that it gives protection against anger and despair, the chief weapons in the devil's armoury.

So I looked again to see what Julian has to say about prayer. I read:

> I am the ground of your beseeching. First it is my will that you should have this. Then I make it your will, too. Then I make you ask for it, and you ask. How then should you not have what you pray for? (Ch. 41)

Clearly people who pray for others in time of trouble – who pray for peace and consolation and understanding and forgiveness – are praying for what it is God's will to give. And, through the tragedy, he has made it their will, too – albeit unexpectedly. The question nags: Does God allow evil to happen simply in order to bring us to our knees?

I thought I had better look again at what Julian says about evil:

> Our blessed Lord answered very gently, with a most kind look, and showed that Adam's sin was the worst harm that was done and ever shall be until the world's end. He also showed this is clearly known by all Holy Church on earth. More than this, he taught me I should look upon the glorious Atonement. For this making amends is more helpful to the salvation of many, without compare, than ever the sin of Adam was harmful.
>
> What our Lord means by this teaching is that we should remember this: 'Since I have brought good out of the worst evil, I want you to know, by this, that I shall bring good out of all lesser evils, too.' (Ch. 29)

Because of Adam's original choice, knowledge of evil is inseparable from the human condition. This is the way things are. But it is also because of Adam's choice that God became man. And if it seems utterly improbable that any good can come out of man killing man, then surely it is even more improbable that any good could come out of man killing God.

But the fact that Christ became man, so that God could know evil by experience, and not only by intelligence, means that every sorrow, every grief, every agony has been experienced by God himself – and that there is no place so dark and painful that God has not been there before us and stays there with us. And the fact of the resurrection means that there is no evil so bad that he cannot turn it into good.

But if this is so – if God has everything in hand, and is going to turn it all into good – I began to wonder why prayer should be necessary. The answer Julian gives is astonishing:

> He looks on us with love and wants to make us his partner in good deeds. As so he leads us to pray for what it is his pleasure to do. And he will reward us and give us endless recompense for these prayers and our good will – which are his gifts to us. God showed such pleasure and such great delight, as if he were much in our debt for every good deed that we do – and yet it is he who does them. And because we ask him eagerly to do the things he loves to do, it is as if he said: 'What could please me better than to ask me – eagerly, wisely and willingly – to do the very thing I am about to do?' And so, by prayer the soul is attuned to God. (Ch. 43)

As if it were not enough – as Julian saw in the story of the Lord and the Servant – that God should take delight in the gifts we bring him, so that he sits waiting on the bare and desert earth until we have carried out the work we have to do, now Julian is shown that God wants 'to make us his partner in good deeds' – to involve us in his own work of redemption.

So I realised that asking why God wants us to pray, had led me to an insight into the nature of the God who wants those prayers. 'God looks on us with love.' And at this point I realised that in spite of all the many times I had heard – and thought I understood – that God looks on us with love, I had always found the idea of God's watchful eye upon me as alarming, rather than reassuring.

On my wall I have two Victorian china plaques, each with a picture of a large disembodied eye. Below this, one has the message: *THOU GOD SEES ME*, while the companion piece warns: *PREPARE TO MEET THY GOD*. Though I can smile at their naiveté, the image of that probing, pitiless, disapproving, disembodied eye, and the fear-stricken piety which it represents still lurks, it seems to me, in the back of our response to God.

But Julian's perception is that God is not just keeping an eye on us and waiting – hoping, even – for the time we put a foot wrong, so he can visit his just wrath upon us. Her perception is that God looks on us with love, and that he delights in us. And he delights in us particularly when we pray:

> Our prayer makes God glad and happy. He wants it and waits for it so that, by his grace, he can make us as like him in condition as we were by creation . . . Our Lord himself is the first to receive our prayer, as I see it. He takes it, full of thanks and joy, and he sends it up above and sets it in the treasury, where it will never be lost. It is there, before God, with all his holy ones – continually heard, continually helping our needs. When we come to heaven, our prayers will be given to us as part of our reward – with endless, joyful thanks from God. (Ch. 41)

Once more, the God who can lack nothing – who has everything, is in everything, does everything – is shown to be the God made needy by love. For although God longs to reward us, he can only give us such gifts as we are capable of receiving. So he yearns for us to pray so that we are able to receive more joy.

For gifts are only worth having if the recipient knows how to use and appreciate them – as unwise parents discover when they give a child a calculator when he would be better off with an abacus. And prayer is the means by which we can gain spiritual strength so that we are able to receive greater gifts of grace. Once more, it seemed amazing to me that so many people think it sane and praiseworthy to spend time and energy keeping physically fit, and regard it as little short of madness to spend time in prayer sustaining spiritual health.

For if, as I have been suspecting, there is both an awareness-of-sin deficiency, and an awareness-of-the-devil deficiency in the world today, then it is absolutely certain that there is also a practice-of-prayer deficiency. And, interestingly enough, a growth of the practice of prayer is one of the first things that has come out of the rediscovery of Julian's book in our time.

Back in 1972, about the time that the celebrations for the 600th anniversary were being planned, I went – with some trepidation – to a day of 'contemplative prayer' in the Prior's Hall of Norwich Cathedral. At the time it seemed a daring and unusual thing to do. For until then I had no idea that praying could mean anything except 'saying prayers'. The day was led by Hilary Wakeman and Pamela Fawcett. The rest is history – for out of their work sprang the Julian Meetings.

This practice of people meeting for silent prayer grew, it seems to me, out of a need. There was an empty space where prayer should have been, and the Julian Meetings arose to fill it. New groups continue to be formed, so that today there are hundreds of Julian groups in this country alone, and many others spread throughout the world.

The result is that contemplative prayer – once the preserve of religious communities – is now regularly practised by thousands of secular people. Most are Christians, but since silence is inclusive, not divisive, people of all faiths, as well as of all denominations, can – and do – meet and pray together. There is no official link between Julian and the Julian Meetings, but when the first groups were being formed and members were asked to suggest a name, time and again it was Julian's name that was put forward. I believe that the rise of the Julian Meetings is a phenomenon as mysterious as the emergence of Julian's own book and is another indication of the power of her writing today.

Another illustration of the way in which Julian's book has helped correct the practice-of-prayer deficiency in our day is the history of a small book called *Enfolded In Love*.

This humble little book of sixty daily readings from The Revelations of Divine Love was published on 8th May 1980 to celebrate Julian's inclusion in the Church of England's Alternative Service Book. It was edited by Robert Llewelyn, illustrated by Irene Ogden and translated – at breakneck speed, at the eleventh hour, when copyright proved an obstacle – by me. The publishers anticipated sales of perhaps 5000. In the event, it has to date sold well over 90,000 copies worldwide and has been translated into half a dozen languages. As well as this, a whole series of daily readings from other great spiritual writers has grown out of it. The purpose of these books is to act as a springboard for prayer – and so the demand for them must indicate that more and more people are prepared to make the dive into its deep and sometimes perilous waters.

For praying does have its perils. It is such a force for good that it is not surprising that there is opposition to it. Evil thoughts can come as well as good ones – and it is also fatally easy to fail to recognise the forces that have an interest in persuading us not to pray – as C.S. Lewis's instructive *Screwtape Letters* point out. One of the most effective ways to do this, is to make people believe their prayers are not heard. And Julian, who spent a lifetime in prayer, and knew its drawbacks as well as its fulfilment, is very encouraging to people struggling with a sense of failure:

So he says this: 'Pray inwardly, even though you find no joy in it. For it does good, even though you feel nothing, see nothing – yes, even though you think you cannot pray. When you are dry and empty, sick and weak, your prayers please me – though there be little enough to please you. All believing prayer is precious to me.' (Ch. 41)

Indeed, it is Julian's admission of her own sense of failure – 'for I have often felt like this myself' – that is such a help to people who are struggling to pray. And so is her ability to see a cause for thanksgiving in everything around her:

It is his will that we should understand that not only does he take care of great and noble things, but also of little and humble things, simple and small – both the one and the other. And this is what he means when he says 'all manner of thing shall be well'. For he wants us to understand that the smallest thing shall not be forgotten. (Ch. 32)

Spiritual giant though she may be, her book is not just for the spiritually advanced. Beginners in belief find she does not wrap up her insights in theological obscurity. There could hardly be a less 'churchy' function to thank God for, than the one she talks about in Chapter 6 – an example so shocking to the sensibilities of the copyists of the Sloane manuscripts that it is omitted altogether:

The goodness of God is the highest prayer that reaches right down to our lowest needs . . . A man walks upright, and the food in his body is sealed as in a well-made purse. When the time of his necessity comes, it is opened and sealed again most properly. And that it is God who does this is shown where he says that he comes down to the lowest part of our need. For he does not despise what he has made, nor does he disdain to serve our humblest earthly needs. For he loves the soul he has made in his likeness.

But for Julian, the truth about prayer is that – eventually – it is not we who pray, but God who prays in us: 'the goodness of God is the highest prayer'. And if God is to pray in us, then our will must become the same as his will – and it is just this transformation that prayer achieves:

First it is my will that you should have this. Then I make it your will, too. Then I make you ask for it, and you ask. How then should you not have what you pray for? (Ch. 41)

But of course we all know that we do not always get what we pray for – because getting what we pray for depends on praying for the right thing. Clearly, if all the conflicting prayers that pour daily from earth to heaven were granted, and God's will was changed to ours, chaos would come again.

But often there are times when we pray for something we are sure it is God's will that we should have – for the gift of grace, of mercy and of peace – and still our prayers do not seem to have been heard. Julian's answer is that our prayers have already been granted, even though we are not aware of it. She writes:

For I am sure that no one can ask for mercy and grace with his whole heart unless mercy and grace have already been given him. Sometimes it seems we have been praying a long time, and still do not have what we ask. But we should not be sad. I am sure what our Lord means by this is that we should wait for a better time, or more grace, or a better gift. (Ch. 42)

It has been my experience – and other people's, too – that prayer *is* answered – and answered, very often, in quite unexpected ways. Time and again I have been given something totally different from the thing I asked for. And time and again, as the years pass, I discover the hidden treasure in the gift, and recognise it as the very thing that, had I had wisdom enough, I should have asked for in the first place.

Discovering God's will, and making ours the same, is the purpose of prayer:

> This is his meaning – that we should see what he does and pray that it should be done. One is not enough without the other. For if we pray and do not see what he is doing, then it makes us sad and full of doubts – and that is no praise to him. And if we see his work and do not pray, then we fail in our duty. And it does no good – that is to say, he does not recognise it. But when we see his work and pray that it shall be done – this honours him and helps us.
>
> It is our Lord's will that, whatever he plans to do, we should pray for it, either in particular or in general. The joy and delight it gives him – and the thanks and glory we shall be given because of it – pass all understanding, as I see it. (Ch. 42)

Praying 'in particular' is easy to understand. It is not even thought strange – even though it is regarded as misguided – by the secular society, since it can be seen to be directed towards a practical outcome. But praying 'in general' is a different matter. The practice of contemplative prayer, which the Julian Meetings have done so much to promote, is viewed with incredulity by the achievement culture, which asks the question: what is contemplative prayer supposed to achieve? Julian's answer is that it achieves nothing less than coming into the presence of God:

> When, by his grace, our courteous Lord shows himself to our

soul, then we have all we desire. And, for the time being, we see nothing more to pray for, but all our mind and strength is gathered up in the sight of him. This is a high, unimaginable prayer in my sight. For all the reasons why we pray are gathered together in looking upon, and seeing, him to whom we pray – rejoicing wonderingly with reverent fear, and with such great joy and delight in him, that for a time we are not able to pray for anything except what he leads us to ask. (Ch. 43)

But this 'high, unimaginable prayer' is not given to many of us most of the time. Nor was it always given to Julian, for she continues:

But when we cannot see him like this, then we have need and cause to pray, because of our failures, to bring ourselves closer to Jesus. For when the soul is tempest-tossed, troubled, and cut off by worries, then is the time to pray – so as to make the soul more responsive towards God. But there is no kind of prayer that can make God more responsive to the soul, for God is always constant in love. (Ch. 43)

Reading this, I was brought back to the church packed with troubled people in the aftermath of tragedy – 'tempest-tossed, troubled, and cut off by worries'. If their prayer brings them closer to God, and to understanding and resting in his love, then already good will be starting to come out of evil. But Julian's most striking insight is that through prayer we become able to perceive that it is not God's response to us that changes, but our response to God. And as our response changes so does our growing awareness of God's love. We discover 'he is always constant in love'.

I believe that prayer is a powerful means of releasing this knowledge of the love of God into the world, and that it has a profound – and unquantifiable – effect. For four years I lived in a house in the grounds of a religious community. There the Sisters, as well as spending time in private prayer, pray together seven times a day, seven days a week – an exercise which, to the secular mind, would seem as pointless as it was self-indulgent. Being on the spot, I was able to see that all this prayer certainly did not mean that the Sisters escaped cares and troubles – either of their own or of the world. They suffered their full share of both. But it seemed to me that through this constant round of prayer, an act of reconciliation was continually being performed – that their prayers kept open a channel through which God's love was able to pour into the world.

Then, as now, King Arthur's words from Tennyson's 'Morte d'Arthur', spoken from the dark barge that will bear him to Avalon, kept coming into my mind:

> but thou
> If thou shouldst never see my face again,
> Pray for my soul. More things are wrought by prayer
> Than this world dreams of. Wherefore let thy voice
> Rise like a fountain for me night and day.
> For what are men better than sheep or goats
> That nourish a blind life within the brain,
> If, knowing God, they lift not hands in prayer
> Both for themselves and those who call them friend?
> For so the whole round world is every way
> Bound by gold chains about the feet of God.

CHAPTER TEN

The Ladies' Room

IT MIGHT SEEM strange to have got so far afield in attempting to find the answer to the question 'Why Julian now?' without so much as opening the door marked 'Ladies' Room'. I had seen it, of course, at the outset, but it seemed to me that it might lead simply into a small room which had no further door opening out on to the long road I was taking. And so I decided to explore further afield first and, if the track led back, return to it later.

I realised, of course, that many other people had gone through that door already. For with the growth of feminism, the work of all sorts of hitherto little-known women is being rediscovered and publicised. And Julian was not merely a woman, but the first woman to write a book in English. This, some people might suppose, is the chief – perhaps the only – reason that we are suddenly hearing all about her today.

If this is the only reason, it looked like a dead end. But, since part of Julian's significance for our day undoubtedly does come from the fact that she is a woman, I obviously had to go through that door. For some reason, I found the prospect distasteful and I knew that, before I stepped over the threshold, I should have to examine the reason for my distaste.

Back in 1963 – ten years before that momentous celebration of Julian's 600th anniversary – I bought a copy of Betty Friedan's newly published *The Feminine Mystique*. I read it with a growing sense of enlightenment. I then went out and bought a second copy and gave it to my old headmistress with instructions – she was not the sort of person you can instruct, but I tried my best – that every girl in the school was to read it.

I did so because it had always irritated me that, whenever I was in a meeting, someone would inevitably turn to me and say: 'And now, perhaps, Sheila, you will give us the woman's point of view.' It irritated me because, while I am very happy to give my opinion on almost anything to anybody, I know perfectly well that its value will come from the fact that I know what works on a stage, or can sail a boat, or keep a dog, or know Middle English, or have been to Australia – or from any of the other assorted bits and pieces of knowledge and experience I have picked up over the years, and not from the fact that I am a woman. And when I read *The Feminine Mystique* I thought that the feminists would open that trap and let me out.

But it was not very long before I discovered that they opened one trap only to shut me fast in another. True, I was no longer expected to know only about arranging flowers or looking after babies – on both which subjects, let's face it, the value of my opinion is zero – but I was now expected, instead, to subscribe to a whole lot of standard opinions on 'women's issues' and 'women's rights'. It was clear to me that, while I might now be perceived to be a different sort of woman, I was still 'women' and not me. And because I find that being dumped into a category is both misleading and demeaning I found myself fighting, on Julian's behalf, against anyone who tried to do the same thing to her.

My belief was – still is – that, as Dorothy L. Sayers points out in her essay *Are Women Human?*,

> A woman is just as much an ordinary human being as a man, with the same individual preferences, and with just as much right to the tastes and preferences of an individual. What is

repugnant to every human being is to be reckoned always as a member of a class and not as an individual person.[1]

So I was determined to consider Julian as a writer who happened to be a woman – not as a woman who happened to be a writer. I wondered how Julian thought of herself. And from the pages of the Short Text – the first version of her book which she probably wrote soon after she had recovered from her near-fatal illness – I found these words staring up at me:

> God forbid that you should say or take it that I am a teacher, for I do not mean that, nor never meant it. I am an unlettered woman, poor and simple. But I know well that, what I say, I have it from the showing of Him who is a mighty teacher – and I tell it to you for love, for I would to God it were known, and my fellow-Christians helped on to greater loathing of sin and loving of God.
>
> Because I am a woman, must I therefore believe that I should not tell you of the goodness of God, when I saw at the same time that it was his will that it should be known? You shall see in what follows if I have understood well and truly. Then shall you soon forget me, who am of no account – and do so, so that I shall not hinder you – and behold Jesus, who is teacher of all. (Short Text. Ch. 1, my translation)

If Julian felt like this about herself, it rather knocked my idea of her as a 'writer who happened to be a woman' on the head. It is a passionate outburst, quite unlike anything else in her exact and controlled writing, and I tried to think what caused it. And then the full significance of that fact 'the first woman to write a book in English' came home to me. At first sight, it seemed a very agreeable thing to have done. If you are the first to climb Everest, to land on the moon, to run a mile in four minutes – or however

---

1. Eerdmans and Paternoster Press, 1971, reprinted 1987, p.19

long it takes these days – it is a personal triumph, and the world applauds. But Julian did not write her book to fulfil a personal ambition and gain acclaim. She wrote it because God commanded her to. She was not attempting something difficult. She was attempting something that most people believed was impossible.

Four hundred years later, Dr Johnson was still raising a laugh about women preaching: 'A woman's preaching is like a dog walking on its hind legs. It is not done well; but you are surprised to find it done at all.' And in fourteenth-century Norwich the possibility of a woman writing a book was far more bizarre than the sight of a dog walking on its hind legs. It was more like an elephant flying. For the obverse of the coin 'The first woman to write a book in English' is the daunting legend: 'No woman has ever written a book in English before'.

Today English is the international language, but in the fourteenth century it was a local dialect. Latin was the international language of scholarship – and everyone agrees that Julian did not know it. The language of diplomacy and of the court was French – and it's very unlikely she knew that, either. English was the peasant's language. It was the working language, the language of the streets. People spoke English when they talked to their servants. English did not even become the official language of England until Julian was twenty years old.

So to be the first woman to write a book in English was hardly an achievement to be proud of. It was another way of saying the first woman foolhardy enough to think she can write a book, even though she has absolutely no qualifications to do so.

Other people had written books in English before, of course, but all of them knew Latin – and all of them were men. Chaucer the diplomat was entrancing the educated with his elegant new frenchified rhyming verse. Langland the priest was writing to attack the corruption in the Church in *Piers Plowman*, still using the old alliterative metre. But they wrote in English because they chose to – not because (unthinkable!) they did not know Latin. It was men who wrote books – men like these – not an uneducated woman living in one room in a backstreet of Norwich.

Knowing all this, Julian must have been filled with a sense of inadequacy almost too huge to contemplate. Walls of ridicule and disbelief must have enclosed her far more claustrophobically than the walls of her cell. I remembered the feeling of inadequacy and loss of self-esteem that can attack people who speak on Julian and imagined this multiplied a thousandfold. And rereading her words 'Because I am a woman, must I therefore believe I should not tell you of the goodness of God', I realised that it was just as wrong for me to want to consider Julian as 'a writer who happened to be a woman' as it was to want to think of her as 'a woman who happened to be a writer'. Julian is a woman and a writer – and an outstanding example of both.

Having got this far, I thought I should try to discover if there were any other disadvantages she had to overcome because she was a woman, and I came to the conclusion that the biggest was that a girl was far less likely than a boy to have been taught to read and write. And not being able to read and write is, surely, a major disqualification when it comes to writing a book. Most scholars, I know, explain her claim that she 'knew no letter' by saying she did not know Latin. But it is my settled belief that, when she was given the task of writing her book, she could not read and write and that she had to sit down and learn her letters before she could begin.

One passage that makes me think this comes in the story of the Lord and the Servant, where she writes, 'Also in this wonderful example I have a key of learning – as it were the beginning of an ABC – by which I can have some understanding of our Lord's meaning' (Ch. 51). And at the end of her book she writes – in her original words, 'And these bene grete things, of which gret things he will we have knowing here as it were in one ABC', which, when I translated it, I expanded slightly to read: 'And he wants us to understand these great things here on earth, as it were in a first reading book, or ABC' (Ch. 80).

Reading this, I realised that the wonderful day when I first discovered that b a t spelt bat and c a t spelt cat is so far behind me that I do not think about it any more. The moments of revelation I remember – like stout Cortez on that peak in Darien – are reading *Alice's Adventures in Wonderland* (and wondering what 'conversations' were), opening *Tales of Classic Heroes* or discovering John Donne. But here we have Julian, who must have been in her forties when she wrote the chapter on the Lord and the Servant, because it appears only in the later Long Text, twice talking about her ABC as the key to understanding, the gateway to knowledge. I can see her sitting across the table from – who knows, perhaps the same 'man of religion' who assured her she was not 'raving' on the day she had her revelations. Between them is a child's reading book – A for apple, B for ball, C for cat – that Julian, the grown woman, had to master before she could start to write her book.

Another reason for my belief that she could not read and write at the time of the Showings is this sentence – perhaps the first she ever wrote – the start of the Short Text (my translation):

I desired three graces by the gift of God. The first was to understand Christ's passion. The second was bodily sickness, and the third was to have, by God's gift, three wounds. As for the first, which came into my mind as I prayed – I thought I already had great feeling for the Passion of Christ, but I wanted to have even more, by the grace of God, for I thought I should have liked to have been there with Mary Magdalen and with the others who were Christ's lovers, so that I might actually have seen the Passion of our Lord, that he suffered for me, so that I was able to suffer with him as the others did that loved him – notwithstanding that I soberly believed in all the pains of Christ, as holy church shows and teaches, and as paintings of the crucifixion also show – that are made by the grace of God, through the teaching of holy church, to show forth Christ's Passion, as far as man's wit can grasp it.

You need to take a deep breath at the end of that. It rattles on and on, clause tacked on to clause, thought on to thought, like the waggons of a goods train, packed with cargo. There's nothing to tell us who she is or what she is talking about – she just plunges in. This sentence in itself, I believe, is further evidence, if any were needed, that Julian wrote her book herself and did not dictate it to a scribe. If she had, he would have been taught his grammar and known how to construct a sentence. He would have tidied it up and made it coherent and manageable.

But by the time she sat down to write the Long Text, Julian's grasp of language is secure and assured:

> These revelations were shown to an unlettered woman in the year of our Lord 1373, on the 8th day of May. This woman had asked for three gifts from God. The first was to understand his Passion; the second was to have an illness in her youth, when she was thirty years old; the third was to have, by God's grace, three wounds. As to the first, I thought I already knew something of Christ's Passion, but I wanted to know even more, by God's grace. I wished I had been there with Mary Magdalen, and those others who were Christ's friends and so I asked for an actual sight – through which I should have more understanding of the compassion of our Lady and all his friends who saw his agony and pain at that time. The reason for this petition was so that afterwards I might have better understanding of the Passion of Christ.

It's crisp, and it's clear, and it's well set out. She tells us who it happened to, when it happened, and why it happened. And I have sympathy with the way that, after starting formally in the third person, 'these revelations were shown to an unlettered woman . . .', she quickly switches into writing in the first person, 'I thought I already knew something of Christ's Passion'. Writing in the third person is a very difficult style to keep up.

But if Julian, because she was a woman, learnt to read and write only in her mid-thirties, and learnt in haste because she had a book to write, it would mean she had time only to learn how to spell the words, not to study the hinterland of grammar. And if she was not able to read before her revelations, she would not have been able to read the few books in English that were available. So she has no literary models, and she writes as she speaks. But, in the way that Julian seems always to be able to turn every disadvantage into an advantage, I believe it is because she could not fetch her style from books that her writing has such freshness and originality – and that it is this freshness and originality that is yet another reason why it is so widely read today.

For Julian had only the everyday spoken English to tell her story. When she wants to find words to describe Christ dying on the cross she can only look round the streets of Norwich:

> The great drops of blood fell down from under the crown of thorns like pellets, as though they burst out of the veins . . . It was as plentiful as the drops of water that fall from the eaves after a great shower of rain, that fall so thick and fast no one can count them. And for roundness, they were like the scale of herring.

This is a woman who lived near the river down King Street, with the rain dripping off the thatch of the merchants' houses on the quayside, and the fish scales thick on the wharves.

Christ's flesh, withering as he died on the cross, she describes like this: 'The skin of the face and body was full of small wrinkles and was a tanned colour, like a dry, scorched board.' And the face the devil thrust near hers 'was very long and thin. I never saw one like it. The colour was red, like new-fired tiles, with black spots on it like freckles, darker than the tile. His hair was red as rust.'

Writing like this is not the work of a woman who is conscious of any inadequacy. It is the work of a born writer working at full stretch. It seemed obvious to me that by the time she wrote the Long Text, Julian had overcome her doubts about her competence, and was no longer concerned with other people's reaction. I wondered if I could find any proof of this. And then I realised that the proof lay, not with what she put in, but with what she left out. In the Long Text the whole of that agonised – and much-quoted – passage 'Because I am a woman must I therefore believe I should not tell you of the goodness of God . . .' has disappeared. All that remains is a simple and necessary warning to heed the message, not the messenger:

> Therefore I pray you all, and I tell you for your own good, that you do not let your eye dwell on the humble woman this was shown to, but let your sight go beyond, and wisely, mightily and humbly behold God who, by his courteous love and endless goodness, wishes it to be widely known to comfort us all.

Julian has forgotten about herself and settled down to tell her story. And, as I read that story, I began to realise that many of the insights in it come from the very fact she thought would make people despise her – the fact she is a woman. And among the sharpest of these insights is what she writes about the motherhood of God.

I realised the path now led into the nursery.

CHAPTER ELEVEN

The Nursery

ANOTHER DOOR I had noticed at the very beginning of my journey was marked 'The Motherhood of God'. But I decided to press on further before I entered it because, like the door of the Duchess's house in *Alice's Adventures in Wonderland*, there was a great deal of noise going on behind it, and from time to time missiles flew out.

One of these, which whizzed past me one day as I was about to speak, was lobbed by an apparently sane, sensible and sober middle-aged woman who asked: 'Do tell me, is it true that Julian of Norwich was the first person to realise that Jesus Christ really was a woman?'

I have also dodged other flying objects, including the claim that Julian says that the first person of the Trinity is female. Indeed at one eucharist in Julian's honour, a voice behind me prayed ostentatiously, 'Our Mother in heaven', and sang 'she' instead of 'he' through all the hymns. I found it hard to believe that we were addressing the same deity – and eventually I decided that I should walk boldly in at that door and explore what Julian actually has to say.

And I found that, in all that she writes of Christ as our mother, Julian never says that the godhead is female. 'He is our mother,' she writes, never 'she is our mother'.

And, of course, if you do set out to think of God as female,

Christ, of all the three persons of the Trinity, is the one who is most obviously a non-starter. It may be possible to pray to 'Our Mother in heaven' without being proved wrong, and some people perceive the Holy Spirit – like Wisdom – to be female. But about Christ's sex there is no doubt at all. It was not a woman who was born at Bethlehem and died on Calvary. It is the male Christ that Julian sees as our mother, and it was this concept that I set out to examine.

It turns up in the book without any preliminaries. She brings the long chapter on the Lord and the Servant to a triumphant conclusion. Then she opens the next in these words:

> And so I saw that God rejoices that he is our father, and God rejoices that he is our mother, and God rejoices that he is our true husband, and the soul his beloved wife. And Christ rejoices that he is our brother, and Jesus rejoices that he is our saviour. (Ch. 52)

That word 'mother' appears in the list unexpectedly – but here she is simply using all the closest human relationships, it seems to me, to express the way that God is all in all to us – much as in an earlier chapter she uses all the five senses to try to express how completely we shall experience God when we finally come to him:

> We shall be enfolded in God forever, seeing him truly, feeling him fully, hearing him spiritually, smelling him delectably and tasting him sweetly. We shall see God face to face, humbly and wholly. (Ch. 43)

But having introduced the word 'mother' almost casually, Julian does not develop the idea of the motherhood of God at this point. She leaves it on one side and goes on to write some of the most profound and complex chapters of her book. She does not return to it until Chapter 57, when she writes:

And so our Lady is our mother, and we are enfolded in her and born of her in Christ. For she who is the mother of our Saviour is also the mother of all who shall be saved by our Saviour. And our Saviour is our true Mother, and we shall be carried within him forever and shall never be born out of him.

The beginning is conventional enough. It is received catholic doctrine that the mother of God is the mother of us all. But in a flash of insight, Julian perceives that this role of mother is too enormous and too important to belong only to our Lady. It is so huge that it can truly be assumed only by Christ himself.

And, if this were not enough for us to grasp, she finds another idea embedded in it. The Church teaches that our Lady became our mother by bearing Christ. But, Julian says, it is not by the act of birth alone that Christ becomes our mother. He is also our mother because we are intimately joined to him: 'We shall be carried within him forever'. He not only bears us, it is also as if he is perpetually pregnant with us.

Of course Julian was not the first writer to speak of Christ as our mother. St Anselm, three hundred years earlier, wrote of St Paul as a mother:

O St Paul, where is he that was called
the nurse of the faithful, caressing his sons?
Who is that affectionate mother that declares everywhere
that she is in labour for her sons?
Sweet nurse, sweet mother,
who are the sons you are in labour with, and nurse,
but those whom by teaching the faith of Christ
you bear and instruct?
who is not born into the faith and established in it by you?
And if in that blessed faith we are born

113

and nursed by other apostles also,
it is most of all by you,
for you have laboured and done more than them all in this:
so if they are our mothers, you are our greatest mother.

And the prayer continues:

And you, Jesus, are you not also like a mother?
Are you not the mother who, like a hen,
gathers her chickens under her wings?
Truly, Lord, you are a mother;
for both they who are in labour
and they who are brought forth
are accepted by you.
You have died more than they, that they may labour to bear.
It is by your death that they have been born,
for if you had not been in labour
you could not have borne death;
and if you had not died, you would not have brought forth.
For, longing to bear sons into life,
you tasted of death,
and by dying you begot them.
You did this in your own self,
your servants by your commands and help.
You as the author, they as the ministers.[1]

Julian would have been aware of the theological ideas and
imagery around her, even if she had not read Anselm – it is unlikely
she had, since he wrote in Latin – and to speak of Christ as our
mother was not breaking new ground. The difference is that when
the celibate monk Anselm, in his cloister, writes about the mother-

---

1. *Prayers and Meditations of St Anselm*, Benedicta Ward (tr.), Penguin, 1973.

hood of Christ he does so, it seems to me, as an intellectual exercise – but when Julian writes, she writes from life.

> Our natural mother, our gracious mother – for he willed wholly to become our mother in all things – humbly and gently found the place to begin his work in the Maiden's womb. And he showed this in the first Showing, where he brought that gentle maid into my mind's eye, at the tender age she was when she first conceived. That is to say, it was in this humble place that our high God, who is the sovereign wisdom of all, set himself to grow, and clothed himself in our poor flesh so that he himself could undertake the work and care of motherhood in all things.
>
> A mother's care is the closest, nearest and surest – for it is the truest. This care never might, nor could, nor should, be fully done except by him alone. We know our own mother bore us only into pain and dying. But our true mother, Jesus, who is all love, bears us into joy and endless living. Blessed may he be! (Ch. 60)

Julian's understanding develops slowly. She begins by seeing that Christ became our mother first of all by taking our nature, then by carrying us within him, and then by looking after us. Now she has another burst of illumination. As she looks on the crucifixion, she sees in it the labour and agony of giving birth, and in Christ's death on the cross she sees a death in childbed.

> And so he nourishes us within himself for love, and he laboured until the full term, because he willed to suffer the sharpest pangs and deepest pains that ever were or ever shall be. And at the end he died. And when he had done this – and so borne us into bliss – yet even all this could not assuage his marvellous love. And he showed this in those high, wonderful

words of love: 'If I could have suffered more, I would have
suffered more.' (Ch. 60)

Here, it seemed to me, that the crippling disadvantage that made
Julian feel that she might never get her book written at all –
the fact that she was a woman – turns into an unforeseen and
unimaginable advantage. The insight that Christ on the cross died
as he bears us into life, as a woman may die in childbirth, is
moving and accurate, and must, I felt sure, spring from experience.

Today childbirth is neither as painful or as dangerous as it used
to be. Not many women still go to be 'churched' and to give thanks
'that thou hast vouchsafed to deliver this woman from the great
pain and peril of Child-birth'. But in fourteenth-century Norwich
childbirth meant, not a sterile delivery room with gas and air, but
women gathered round the family bed in a dark room under the
thatch, and the mother crying out in agony. Julian may well have
been at one of those tragic births where the baby lived and the
mother died.

Time and again she uses her ordinary, everyday knowledge, and
her ordinary, everyday words, to illuminate a theological point in
a way that a formal education would surely have beaten out of
her. She uses the things she knows about to tell us of God's love
– the scale of herring, the raindrops falling from the eaves, a
mother's love – and she uses them in a way that goes straight to
our hearts.

> He could die no more, but he would not cease from working.
> And so he needs must feed us. For the dear love of mother-
> hood has given him a duty to us. A mother feeds her child
> with her milk, but our beloved Mother, Jesus, feeds us with
> himself. He feeds us courteously and tenderly with the Blessed
> Sacrament – which is the precious food of life itself ... A
> mother can lean her child tenderly on her breast, but our
> tender mother Jesus can lead us simply into his blessed breast

116

through his dear wounded side ... This dear and lovely word
'mother' is so sweet, and so true to itself, that it cannot properly be said of anyone but of him, and of she who is the true
mother of us all. (Ch. 60)

This intimacy with motherhood, it seemed to me, is not the
observation of an outsider, and, in spite of Julian's warning 'do
not let your eye dwell on the humble woman this was shown to',
it seemed to me it was necessary to consider the writer along with
her work if I was to explore what makes her book so popular
today. Most early editors of Julian's book supposed her to be a
nun – and that her image of Christ our mother came from her own
happy childhood. It was Sr Benedicta Ward, giving the Julian
lecture in 1988 (later published as *Julian Reconsidered*)[2] who opened
my eyes:

When Julian was a child of 6, the Black Death reached Norwich
and a third of the population died ... The instinctive reaction
after great disasters is towards marriage and childbearing. It
was in just such a situation that Julian grew up and no one was
to know that the plague would return. At marriageable age
[14 or 15] it is most unlikely that Julian herself would have
remained unmarried and there is no reason to suppose that she
herself wished for anything else. The realities of the fourteenth
century meant that fifty was the usual limit of life and thirty
was middle age, by which time a woman should have been
married for at least fifteen years ... If it could be permissible
to suppose her to have borne at least one child, as married
women should, all the language of motherhood takes on a
new and natural meaning. Can one go further and suggest
that a child, loved and watched and guarded in his way, had
died, perhaps in one of the onslaughts of the plague? In 1361,

---

2. SLG Press, 1988

when Julian would have been 19, a form of plague occurred which was especially fatal to young children. Had her young husband died in either plague or in war? . . . and perhaps her child or children died too?

If this is so, and it has the ring of truth, then Julian brings all her experience as a wife, as a mother, as a widow – and as a woman who has had to watch her children die, to illuminate God's love for us. She is not inventing a new feminist theology, but speaking from the heart in the only language she knows.

A kind loving mother, who knows and understands the needs of her child, looks after it tenderly as is her way and nature. As it grows bigger she changes her ways, but not her love. And when it grows older still she allows it to be spanked to break it from vice and lead it to goodness and grace. And our Lord does the same thing, truly and well, to those he brings up. (Ch. 60)

Certainly Julian knows about children, especially in that word spanked – which might get her into trouble in some places today. Her original word is 'bristined', and some translations give it as 'beaten'. This sounded too heavy-handed to me, and since I thought 'bristined' sounded like a swift slap, I used the word 'spanked'. She goes on:

A mother may sometimes let her child fall and be unhappy in many ways for its own good. But she will never allow any real harm to come to the child because of the love she bears it. And though an earthly mother may have to allow her child to die, our heavenly mother Jesus will not allow any one of us who is his child to perish. For he is all power, all wisdom and all love – and no one is but he. Blessed may he be! (Ch. 61)

I can't help sensing in those words 'an earthly mother may have to allow her child to die' that Julian had indeed watched beside her own child's deathbed. But her insight goes beyond the fact that a mother will sometimes let her child suffer for its own good. It is that the God who does the same goes on loving us even while we are sinning – that God our Father loves us like a mother:

> But often, when our falling and miserable sin is shown to us, we are so ashamed we scarcely know where to put ourselves. But our loving mother does not want us to run away from him then, for he does not love us less. But he wills that we behave as children do. For when they are unhappy and frightened they run quickly to their mother for help, with all their might, saying this: 'My own mother, my dear mother, please pity me. I have made myself unclean and unlike you, and I cannot heal myself without your special help and grace.' And if we do not begin to feel better straight away, we can be sure he is behaving like a wise mother. For if he sees it is better for us to sorrow and weep, he allows us to be sad for a while, pitying us and sorrowing with us, for love. (Ch. 61)

Of course we know that the God who made all things is not 'a man' – and in the story of the Lord and the Servant Julian, ever meticulous, makes this clear: 'Whenever he, in his goodness, shows himself to man, he shows himself homely – as a man. Notwithstanding I did not see him wholly, we ought to know and believe that the Father is not a man.' (Ch. 51). But we have to use words to try to express the inexpressible – the God who is alpha and omega, the beginning and the end, beyond male and female. And it is Julian, the unlettered woman, who has the courage to lay hold on words and stretch them to their limit.

We respond so eagerly to what she writes about the motherhood of God, I believe, because she shows us that the fierce bewhiskered

God with the impossibly high standards – who is waiting for us to put a foot wrong so he can thrash us with the cane he keeps behind his study door – is nothing but our own invention. She shows us, instead, an image of God who can, perhaps, be understood in terms of today's fathers – men who are happy to hug their children, to play games, push prams and change nappies without feeling that their manhood is thereby somehow diminished; fathers who are allowed to show warmth and compassion, to shed tears.

But the promise of that loving father is not that this life will be an earthly Paradise. We shall be tempest-tossed and work-worn, we shall be blind and in the dark. But the assurance God gave Julian and which she, in her intimate and homely language, passes on to us, is that though we lose sight of him, he does not lose sight of us, and that, whatever befalls us, he holds us securely – and that always and forever we are children of his love.

This poem by Frank J. Exley, which Sue Ryder takes as the title of her autobiography, sums it up.

Child of My Love

Child of my love fear not the unknown morrow
Dread not the new demands life makes of thee.
Thine ignorance doth hold no cause for sorrow
For what thou knowest not is known to me.

Thou canst not see today the hidden meaning
Of my command, but thou the light shalt gain.
Walk on in faith upon my presence leaning
And as thou goest all shall be made plain.

One step thou seest, then go forward boldly.
One step is far enough for faith to see.

Take that, and thy next duty will be shown thee
For step by step thy Lord is leading thee.

Stand not in fear, thine adversaries counting
Dare every peril – save to disobey.
Thou shalt march on, all obstacles surmounting
For I, the strong, will open up the way.

Therefore go boldly to the task assigned thee
Having my promise, needing nothing more
Save this – to know, where'er the future find thee
In all thy journeyings I go before.

CHAPTER TWELVE

A Fellow Traveller

IT WAS WHEN I had reached this stage in my journey I decided to thumb a lift. Among the papers on my desk was a brochure listing a retreat on Julian of Norwich and Teresa of Avila. Needing to seek a saint, I signed up – intending, I may say, to spend more time in Julian's company than in Teresa's.

I might have known that so formidable a saint as Teresa would not let herself be sidelined – particularly since the retreat was in a Priory of Discalced Carmelites, the order she herself founded. For it was to be Teresa who gave me yet another answer to my question 'Why Julian now?'

To begin with, as I read Teresa's *Interior Castle* for the first time, I was struck, time and again, by how often she said the same thing as Julian:

> *Reflecting, we realise that the soul of a just person is nothing else but a Paradise where the Lord finds his delight.* (*Interior Castle*, Ch. 1, I)[1]

Then our good Lord opened my eyes and showed me my soul

---

1. All extracts from Teresa of Avila's writing used in this chapter are taken from Vol. 2 of Kavanaugh and Rodriguez, *Collected Works of St Teresa*, ICS, 1980.

in the depths of my heart. I saw it was as big as an endless world, and like a blessed kingdom. (Ch. 67)

Then if you should at times fall, don't become discouraged and stop striving to advance, for even from this fall God will draw out good ... Even if we didn't see our misery – or the great harm that a dissipated life does to us – through any other means than through this assault that we endure for the sake of being brought back to recollection, that would be enough. (Interior Castle, Ch. 2, 2)

And after this he allows some of us to fall harder and more painfully than we ever did before, it seems to us. And then we – who do not know everything – think that all our work is wasted. But it is not so. We need to fall, and we need to see we have fallen. For if we never fell, we should never know how poor and weak we are on our own – nor should we ever fully know the wonderful love of our Maker. (Ch. 61)

We ... should not abandon prayer, which is what the devil wants us to do. For the most part all the trials and disturbances come from our not understanding ourselves. (Interior Castle, Ch. IV, 1.9)

When the soul is tempest-tossed, troubled and cut off by worries, then is the time to pray (Ch. 43) ... and all our troubles come because our own love fails us. (Ch. 37).

The Lord, it seems, gives the devil licence so that the soul might be tried and even be made to think it is rejected by God. (Interior Castle, Ch. VI, 1.10)

It is by his permission that we are tested in the Faith by our soul's enemy, and made strong. (Ch. 70)

It seemed to me that these two remarkable women were talking

123

about God in the same way. Certainly they give the same advice about visionary experiences, practically word for word.

> *One thing I advise you; do not think, even if the locutions are from God, that you are better because of them ... All the good comes from how one benefits by these words.* (*Interior Castle*, Ch. VI, 3.5)

> Because of this showing I am not good. I am only good if I love God better. If you love God better than I do because of it, it does you more good than me. (Ch. 40)

And yet, in the end, I found it was the differences between them, and not the similarities, that opened my eyes. I had hardly got two pages into *Interior Castle* before I read:

> *Just as it doesn't do us any harm to reflect on things that are in heaven and what the blessed enjoy – but rather rejoice and strive to attain what they enjoy – it doesn't do us any harm to see that it is possible in this exile for so great a God to commune with such vile-smelling worms.* [*Interior Castle*, Ch. 1, 3]

'Vile-smelling worms'. It was utterly impossible that Julian could ever have used these words to describe souls that are loved by God. She writes:

> For our soul is so deep rooted in God, and so endlessly treasured, that we cannot come to know it until we first know God, its Maker to whom it is joined. But even so I saw we must, to be complete, desire wisely and truly to know our own soul. And by this we are taught to seek it where it is – and that is, in God. (Ch. 56)

Teresa, too, writes about knowing ourselves through knowing God in a very similar passage. But she does not say that contemplating God will bring recognition of how much we are loved – only that it will show us our imperfections:

124

In my opinion we shall never completely know ourselves if we don't strive to know God. By gazing at his grandeur, we shall get in touch with our own lowliness; by looking at his purity, we shall see our own filth; by pondering his humility, we shall see how far we are from being humble. (*Interior Castle*, Ch. 1, 9)

These 'vile worms' and this 'filth' are a world away from Julian's vision of the soul God loves and has made in his likeness. But I then reflected that, when she wrote the *Interior Castle* in 1577 – some 200 years after Julian's Showings – Teresa was giving the official view of the Catholic Church of her day. She had to. The Church was under threat. Protestantism was flaring all over Europe. Luther had broken with Rome when Teresa was four years old. When she was a nineteen-year-old novice Henry VIII – though still a Catholic – had broken from Rome, and he and all England had been excommunicated four years later.

Heresy was to be stamped out at all costs and the Inquisition in Spain was committed to seek and destroy any form of unorthodoxy, particularly heresy in books. The Index of Forbidden Books was published in 1547, when Teresa was thirty-two, before she had written any of her major works. Each of her books had to be referred to the censors, who not only instructed her to alter them but made alterations themselves. A complaint from an embittered ex-nun (a widowed princess who had been allowed to enter the convent when pregnant with her last child) was enough to prompt the Inquisition to call in all existing copies of Teresa's *Life* and subsequently 'lose' them in their voluminous files until after her death – and this in spite of the fact that the book had already been thoroughly examined, amended and approved by the censor.

Teresa's books came under special scrutiny, too, because she was a woman, for women were suspect in seventeenth-century Spain, particularly if they claimed to have spiritual gifts. Many theologians feared that contemplative prayer – which Teresa taught her nuns – could lead to Protestantism and that it was, in any case, unsuitable for women, who should be content with the Our Father and the Hail Mary. The Chief Inquisitor, Fernando Valdez – in a passage that with hindsight is rich in humour – complained that one of his colleagues was trying to write things about contemplation for 'mere carpenters' wives'. He might have chosen his words more carefully had he stopped to consider that it was, after all, a carpenter's wife who had replied 'Let it be' to the angel – and that she, at least, had some claim to know what contemplative prayer was about.

But because of the antagonism towards women that surrounded her, Teresa continually puts herself down: 'I realised I was a woman and wretched and incapable of doing any of the useful things I desired to do in the service of the Lord' (*Way of Perfection,* Ch. 3, no. 1). 'Learned and wise men know about these things very well, but everything is necessary for our womanly dullness of mind' (*Interior Castle,* Ch. 1, 6).

She makes a parade of her submission to male authority. She writes of her confessor:

> *He was a very spiritual man and a theologian with whom I discussed everything about my soul. And he discussed these matters with other learned men, among whom was Father Mancio. They found that none of my experiences was lacking in conformity with Sacred Scripture. This puts me very much at peace now, although I understand that as long as God leads me by this path I must not trust myself in anything. So I have always consulted others, even though I find it difficult. (Spiritual Testimonies, 3. No. 13)*

But somehow it seemed to me that most of this grovelling – unlike Julian's passionate outburst 'Because I am a woman . . .' – was a necessary defence, not a cry from the heart. Indeed, when Teresa did write passionately in *Way of Perfection* about the way

women were treated by the Church, she was promptly told to edit
it out. The whole of the passage in brackets was censored:

> *Nor did you, Lord, when you walked in the world, despise women:*
> *rather, you always, with great compassion, helped them. [And you*
> *found as much love and more faith in them than you did in*
> *men. Among them was your most blessed mother, and through her*
> *merits – and because we wear her habit – we merit what, because*
> *of our offences, we do not deserve. Is it not enough, Lord, that the*
> *world has so intimidated us so that we may not do anything worth-*
> *while for you in public, or dare speak some truths that we lament*
> *over in secret . . . Since the world's judges are sons of Adam and all*
> *of them men, there is no virtue in women that they do not hold*
> *suspect. Yes, indeed, the day will come, my King, when everyone*
> *will be known for what he is. I do not speak for myself . . . but*
> *because I see that these are times in which it would be wrong to*
> *undervalue virtuous and strong souls, even though they are women.]*
> *(Way of Perfection, Ch. 3, no. 7)*

Just how undervalued these virtuous and strong souls were is
clear from this advice by Francis de Osuna, written in 1531 – the
year Teresa entered a convent.

> Since you have seen your wife going about visiting many
> churches, practising many devotions, and pretending to be a
> saint, lock the door; and if that isn't sufficient, break her leg
> if she is young, for she can go to heaven lame from her own
> house without going around in search of these suspect forms
> of holiness. It is enough for a woman to hear a sermon and
> then put it into practice. If she desires more, let a book be read
> to her while she spins, seated at her husband's side.[1]

---

1. Quoted in Vol.2 of Kavanaugh and Rodriguez, *Collected Works of St Teresa*,
ICS, 1980, p.22

Fourteenth-century England, where the Wife of Bath set off merrily for Canterbury, and Margery Kempe travelled unescorted to Rome and the Holy Land was a very different place for women than seventeenth-century Spain.

But, thinking of the constraints that fettered St Teresa, I became acutely aware of what the consequences of Julian's apparent unorthodoxy would have been if her views had reached official ears. She would have been burnt at the stake and her book thrown on the fire along with her. It was all very well for Julian to claim that she was not led away from the Church's teaching at any point by the Showings – and all very well for me, writing in 1997, to try to show that what she writes is in fact consistent with her claim – but not many people in the ecclesiastical establishment in fourteenth-century Norwich would have agreed. I let a few of Julian's phrases run through my mind:

> In God there is no anger, as I see it. . . . He looks on his servants with pity, not with blame. . . . I saw our Lord put no more blame upon us than upon his Son, beloved Christ. . . . I saw that sin has no substance or manner of being, but is only known by the pain it causes. . . . Our inborn will is to have God, and the goodwill of God is to have us. . . . For I saw no anger except on man's part, and God forgives this anger in us. . . . There is no hell except sin for a soul that is true to its nature. . . . God showed that sin shall not be a shame to man, but a glory. . . . The mark of sin shall be turned to honour.

Recalling all this in the light of the censorship of Teresa's books, I realised for the first time that I had in my hands, not a soothing volume of holy thoughts, but a book, were its meaning to be misinterpreted, that could be taken for red-hot heresy. As I skimmed through it, I realised there was scarcely a line of it that would be passed for fourteenth-century publication. I remembered Brian Thorne's suggestion that the reason there are so few manuscript copies of her book is because only a few were made – and those few were passed round secretly among trusted friends. That must be true. My own idea, that most copies were lost at the Dissolution, was wide of the mark. I marvelled again at Julian's courage. And I marvelled at the courage of her friends and at the support and loyalty they must have given her. They, too, would have been sent to the stake if they had been discovered with a copy of her book.

So yet another answer to that question 'Why Julian now?' seems to be that it is because our grip on dogma has slackened enough for us to be able to listen to what she says without feeling threatened by it. For today the threat to Christendom is not 'the Lollards', as in Julian's day, nor the 'Protestants', as in Teresa's. The Albigensian heresy and the filioque controversy are no longer matters for burning. We are beginning to understand that God is not altered or demeaned if we sometimes make mistakes about him. And we are also coming to realise that it can even be better to make mistakes, and learn from them, than to cling blindly on to what we know, for fear of losing everything. The threat to Christendom today is from forces of evil outside the Church, not from differences of opinion within it. And Julian's book unites those who recognise evil, and who arm themselves to fight against it.

For one of the great graces that has been given to the Church in our day is that Christians are becoming aware, more and more, of what joins them rather than of what divides them. Julian, I know, has played a part in this. I have been asked to talk about Julian by Methodists, Orthodox, Anglicans, Roman Catholics and URC – and by many people who have not signed up for any particular denomination or even religion, but who are wanting to know the answer to that question 'Why Julian now?'. Everywhere people are united by her book – united by the love that flows out of it. 'What can make me love my fellow Christians more,' Julian writes, 'than to see that God loves all who shall be saved as if they were just one soul.' (Ch. 38)

And so the answer Teresa of Avila gave me to my question 'Why Julian now?' is, once more, the answer I suspected from the beginning – that it is because her century and ours are, not similar, but completely different from each other. But this time, the comparison is in our favour. Today, by the grace of God, our suspicion and hostility towards fellow Christians whose beliefs are not identical to ours are being laid aside, so we can greet each other as friends and not as enemies. It is an answer that would rejoice Julian's heart, and it echoes her words:

> When I think of myself joined in love with all my fellow Christians, I have hope, for in this joining lies the life of all who shall be saved.

TAILPIECE

AS I EMPTIED out my bag at the end of the voyage, something tumbled out. It was a little thing, the size of a hazelnut, that I had carried with me all through my journey. I remembered Julian's words:

> And then he showed me a little thing, the size of a hazelnut, in the palm of my hand, and it was as round as a ball. I looked at it with my mind's eye and I thought: 'What can this be?' And the answer came 'It is all that is made.' I marvelled that it could last, for I thought it might suddenly have crumbled to nothing, it was so small. And the answer came into my mind: 'It lasts and ever shall, because God loves it.' And so all things have being through the love of God.

Why, I wondered, should so many people remember the image of the hazelnut when they think of Julian. Did it hold another answer to the question 'Why Julian now?'? Was there any special reason why this 'little thing' should mean so much to us today? And then alongside Julian's lines I set these – written by the astronaut Russell Schweickart – in which a modern man who has orbited the earth, and a mediaeval woman who never left her cell, use practically the same words:

> And a little later on your friend goes to the moon. And now

131

he looks back and sees the Earth not as something big, where he can see the beautiful details, but now he sees the Earth as a small thing out there. And the contrast between that bright blue-and-white Christmas tree ornament and the black sky, that infinite universe, really comes through, and the size of it, the significance of it. It is so small and so fragile and such a precious little spot in the universe that you can block it out with your thumb, and you realise that on that small spot, that little blue-and-white thing, is everything that means anything to you – all of history and music and poetry and art and death and birth and love, tears, joy, games, all of it on that little spot out there that you can cover with your thumb. And you realise from that perspective that you've changed, and there is something new there, that the relationship is no longer what it was.

After looking through Julian's eyes, our relationship with God, with the universe, and with ourselves, is no longer what it was. Our eyes are focused to a different vision. And, slowly, we come to have faith that we are created and sustained by love, and that through God's great deed, and in God's good time.

> All shall be well,
> and all shall be well, and
> all manner of thing shall be well.